How to Write Effective Business English

How to Write Effective Business English

The essential toolkit for composing powerful letters, e-mails and more, for today's business needs

Fiona Talbot

KOGAN PAGE

London and Philadelphia

Publisher's note

Every possible effort has been made to ensure that the information contained in this book is accurate at the time of going to press, and the publishers and author cannot accept responsibility for any errors or omissions, however caused. No responsibility for loss or damage occasioned to any person acting, or refraining from action, as a result of the material in this publication can be accepted by the editor, the publisher or the author.

First published in Great Britain and the United States in 2009 by Kogan Page Limited

120 Pentonville Road	525 South 4th Street, #241
London N1 9JN	Philadelphia PA 19147
United Kingdom	USA
www.koganpage.com	

© Fiona Talbot, 2009

The right of Fiona Talbot to be identified as the author of this work has been asserted by her in accordance with the Copyright, Designs and Patents Act 1988.

ISBN 978 0 7494 5520 0

British Library Cataloguing-in-Publication Data

A CIP record for this book is available from the British Library.

Library of Congress Cataloging-in-Publication Data

Talbot, Fiona.
    How to write effective business English : the essential toolkit for composing powerful letters, emails and more, for today's business needs / Fiona Talbot. -- 1st ed.
      p. cm.
    ISBN 978-0-7494-5520-0
    1. English language--Business English--Study and teaching 2. Business communication--Study and teaching 3. English language--Textbooks for foreign speakers. 4. Business writing. I. Title.
    PE1479.B87T35 2009
    808'.06665--dc22
                                                2009016900

Typeset by JS Typesetting Ltd, Porthcawl, Mid Glamorgan
Printed and bound in India by Replika Press Pvt Ltd

Dedication

I would like to thank my family, friends and clients for their support throughout my career. It is a wonderful fact that, by sharing experiences and lessons learnt, we all learn from each other, to our mutual benefit.

Special thanks must go to my dear husband, Colin. I would like to dedicate this series to him – and to my son, Alexander, and my daughter, Hannah-Maria. And to my mother, Lima.

Contents

Preface

How this series works – and what it is about

There are three books in the series, designed to improve your confidence and competence in writing English for global business. They are designed on three levels, to fit in with the three stages in the business cycle.

My central philosophy is this: writing business English effectively for international trade is about creating clear, concise messages and avoiding verbosity. But the fewer words you write, the more important it is that you get them right.

Book 1: How to Write Effective Business English

This book assumes that you know English to intermediate level and provides effective guidelines. It deals with real-life scenarios, to give you answers that even your boss may not know.

It uses a system that also gives you the building blocks to take you to the next level in the cycle of success, set out in Book 2.

Book 2: Make an Impact with your Written English

This book will take you a further step forward in your executive career.

You will learn how to use written word power to promote and sell your messages, as well as 'brand you'. You will learn how to make your mark writing English, whether for PR, presentations, reports, meeting notes, manuals etc. And for cyberspace, where English is today's predominant language.

You will learn how to deal with pressing challenges that you need to be aware of. And how to write English that impresses, so that you get noticed for the right reasons.

Book 3: Executive Writing Skills for Managers

This book deals with the English business writing you need at the top of your career and focuses on writing as a key business tool.

It gives amazingly valuable tips on harmonizing the English that you and your teams use (for example, for evaluation performance) – tips that you quite simply have not seen before. It also introduces the concept of Word Power Skills 2.0 – for unified English business writing that keeps everyone in the loop.

The importance of business English today

Increasingly, English language is the language of choice used in multinational gatherings. It may not be the predominant language of the group, but is the most likely to be understood by the majority – at least at a basic level – so becomes a powerful tool for communication and inclusion.

You may have to unlearn some things you learnt at school

Writing English for business today is highly unlikely to be the same as the writing you were taught at school or university. Apart from getting your punctuation and grammar right, the similarities often end there.

This series works with the business cycle

The series highlights the essential role business writing plays at every stage in your career path – and alongside the cycle of business in general. Figures 1 and 2 show how this works. I describe below how it relates to the three phases.

Phase one: joining an organization or setting up your own business

English business writing needs at the outset of your career: a CV, letter, job application, start-up plan or business plan, routine business writing tasks.

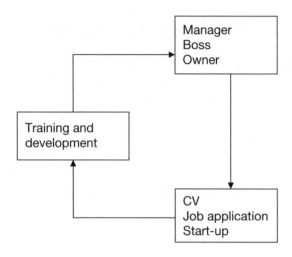

Figure 1 The business cycle: from the individual's perspective

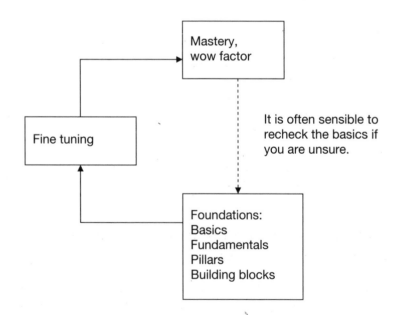

Figure 2 The business cycle: from the business writing perspective

As you start your career, you need to understand how to get the basics right. You need to understand how to write correctly, how spelling, punctuation and grammar matter. You will not get to the next phase in your career – the pitching phase – without getting the basics right.

Phase two: you develop through knowing how to harness word power

Your developing English business writing needs; making impact in everything you write in English; personal self-development or other training.

Great business English writing will generate ideas and sparks that capture readers' attention and take your career forward. Powerful writing can sell your proposals so well – weak writing can do the exact opposite.

Phase three: mastery of written word power enables you to shine and lead

English business writing needs at the height of your career: mastery of written word power required for leadership, to shine as a manager, boss and/or owner.

You do not get to the top by blending in. You have to build bridges, shape outcomes and lead through word power. You need to express your ideas in writing – so use business English that makes readers want to buy in.

The series is an easy, indispensable, comprehensive guide

It is an essential tool kit to keep by your desk or take on your travels. Dip in and out of it as and when you need the answers it provides, to help you shine in all stages of your career.

So each of the three books aligns with the business cycle and supports your development and perfection of writing English for business to gain the competitive edge – because the development of the written word goes hand in hand with, or even is, the business cycle itself.

Get results!

Just take a look at my methods, focus on the elements that apply to your business writing and make sure they become an intrinsic part of your real-life performance.

This series does not take you away from your job: it focuses on your job and uses word power as a free resource. All you have to do is harness this – and enjoy the benefits of immediate results and sustainable improvements.

Good luck on your journey to success!

Fiona Talbot
TQI Word Power Skills
www.wordpowerskills.com

Introduction

This book is an essential guide to keep with you, by your desk or on your travels. It provides a wealth of answers to help you impress.

Look on it as your introduction to being the best! By the time you reach the end, you will be more confident and more competent in writing English. You will be developing a key transferable skill, because English is the global business language of today.

1

Why you need to write

Defining readers, customers and audience

Throughout this book I use the terms readers, target readership, customers and audience interchangeably. I use 'customer' both in its most common usage as a person who buys goods or services from a business, and in the broadest sense of signifying a person that you deal with in the course of your daily work. So the term applies just as much to internal colleagues, suppliers, those in the public sector etc as it does to those who are external buying consumers.

Your audience can be anyone and everyone

I use many practical examples and scenarios in this book that relate to standard sales or customer pitches. Because we are all consumers in our private lives, we can easily relate to and understand these examples. What I would like to stress is that the concepts apply equally to every scenario in the list that follows. Think of lobbying; think of politics; think of charities; think of fundraising; think of promotions.

Why we write in business

People sometimes think of business writing as a 'soft' skill. In fact, you may see communication generally classified as a soft skill, as opposed to the 'hard' skills of finance, law, IT etc. But I think this description is misleading. After all, people drive processes. And how do they do this? By communication. The label 'soft' can give the impression that business writing is an easy option, which it certainly is not. Business writing can impact on the whole business cycle; it can win business, it can lose business and it can communicate the framework by which results can be achieved.

This is why, at the outset of my training workshops, I always take time to ask people why they actually write in their job and what outcomes they seek, individually and as teams. I ask my clients to write down why they need to write in their businesses. And the following aspects of business writing always come top of the list:

- to inform or record;
- to cascade information;

- for compliance;

- to seek information;

- to write specifications;

- to achieve a standard;

- to write reports with recommendations;

- to persuade;

- to promote services.

Usually far lower on the list (and sometimes only when prompted by me, on the lines of 'Aren't there any other reasons?'), they record such things as:

- to engage interest and involve;

- to get the right results;

- to sell;

- to support customers;

- to improve life for customers;

- to eat, breathe and live our vision.

Notice how the most inspirational aspects of writing are the ones that are listed as an afterthought.

Why is this? Maybe companies need to focus more on how powerful business writing can be and how their employees need to think creatively about how best to harness this virtually free resource. Think about what writing really means for your company and which aspects of your business it covers.

Readers judge writing for what it is

There is no doubt: the written word is unforgiving. When I read, I judge what I see written for what it is. If I am looking for products or services, what I see can be what I think I get. If it is your writing, I will judge both you as an individual and your company on the basis of how you expressed yourself at that point in time.

It is amazing how many written messages can lead to confusion and misunderstanding – even when a company is writing in its native language. Poor writing can also lead to customer complaints. At the least, these complicate relations with customers – even though we may still be able to convert a complaint to a positive experience.

The worst scenarios are where customers walk away from the companies concerned, and tell others about the bad experience they have received or think they have received. That is the impact that ineffective writing can have. It becomes quite clear that if, as customers, we do not understand or like what supplier A is writing, we prefer to buy from supplier B, who cares enough about our needs to get the message right. And if this takes less time, so much the better.

No body language signals in writing

When we communicate face to face, people around us attach a lot of importance to the signals given by our body language. These are said to account for 55 per cent of the impact we make when giving a talk. Our voice can account for perhaps 38 per cent – and our words just 7 per cent.

This is because, in face to face communication, unlike writing, we do not need to focus just on words. We can ask if we are not sure what is being said. We can look for clues from the speaker's facial expression or tone as to the gravity or levity of the subject matter. These will help our understanding and focus our attention (or not!).

But with writing, unless the writer is there in front of you, time will elapse before you can get the answers to any questions you have. That is, if you have the time or inclination to ask questions. At the very least, it means that writers need to think twice, spellcheck – in fact, double-check – that their words are saying what they mean them to say.

A state of flux

Business writing is in a state of flux. So is the way English is used in business, as I discuss in Chapter 3. One thing you will notice as a direct result is that business writing in English is becoming increasingly diverse in style. Different styles may even coexist within the same company. It can be bewildering for reader and writer alike. Generally speaking, the move in business English writing is not only towards more 'people' words, but also towards more informality.

This can be a special challenge for cultures that place great emphasis on hierarchy, where people of senior grades are treated with noticeably more deference and respect than those in junior grades. Informality can also be a challenge for nationalities where there is a distinction between a familiar and a formal form of the pronoun 'you'. As an example, French makes a distinction between '*tu*' (informal) and '*vous*' (formal), as does German with '*du*' and '*Sie*'. Such cultures can try to compensate for this lack of distinction by writing more elaborately for what they see as the 'formal you' as opposed to the 'informal you'. This does not necessarily work.

Your checklist for action

- Recognize writing as a fundamental skill for you as an individual and for your business.

- Develop and improve your writing at every opportunity throughout your career.

- Remember that English business writing – in its many forms – is your most common route to market. Be the best.

2

Defining business English

English is a major language of commercial communication. It is also the world's language of the internet and of global access to knowledge. Business English is the name given to the English used for dealing with business communication in English – though you will find many variants, as I will shortly explain. This can present unexpected problems unless you understand how to design your communication to give you the best chance of success, whatever the variety of business English used by your target audience.

'Standard' and 'variant' English

A particularly interesting fact is that there are more non-native speakers of English than native English speakers. As I write, the UK government estimates that more than 1 billion people speak English, and projections indicate that by 2020 2 billion people worldwide will be learning or teaching English. So we can see that English is certainly no longer the preserve of the nation that gives the language its name. It belongs to no single culture; instead it is something that acts as a bridge across borders and cultures.

Years ago when I first worked abroad, I saw the commercial need to help multinationals seize the competitive edge in their use of English as a global business language. It was then that I realized how puzzled both foreigners and native English speakers can be by the way English is used. Often it is because non-native English speakers use it in unconventional ways. It is also often because people do not realize that UK or British English is not exactly the same as the many other variations of business English that exist. These include US or American English, Australian English, Caribbean English, Indian English, Irish English, Singapore English and South African English. You can see how extensive the list is.

Business communication is crucial to success. So if people are puzzled by that communication, this will have an adverse effect on results. We cannot pretend this does not matter, because getting the right messages out and receiving the right answers are the lifeblood of commercial success. I found it helped my clients communicate effectively cross-culturally when I showed them how to follow some norms of commonly accepted 'standard' English. This not only helped mutual comprehension but also secured buy-in to their business objectives, from internal as well as external customers.

So what is meant by 'standard' English? I use the expression to mean the English routinely described in mainstream English dictionaries and grammar books. To describe the many variants of English, such as those I have mentioned, is clearly outside the remit of this series. Naturally you and your company will know which you will wish to use at any one time. By and large, it is true to say that the standard English I use throughout this book is likely to be intelligible to users of the other variants.

I do need to mention at the outset that, unless I indicate otherwise, the spelling and grammar used in the series are the UK English variety requested by my publishers, to follow their house style. One of the challenges in writing UK English is that there can be more than one correct way of spelling certain words. Just to list a few examples: recognize and recognise, minimize and minimise, judgment and judgement, e-mail and email can all be used correctly in UK English. Some people give explanations for these differences that are too simplistic, saying that 'recognize' indicates an American English spelling. But this is only part of the picture – and you will find more on variant spellings later in the book.

So there are times when I may refer to US English as well, where there are clearly divergent spellings or meanings. It is, however, beyond the remit of this series to highlight spelling and grammatical differences between UK and US English in comprehensive detail.

This observation takes me to my next point. Whenever we write and whatever we write, we must understand the conventions we need to follow, if we are to please our target readers. This has to be the best starting point from a business perspective. If necessary, explain at the outset the convention you are following, so that you avoid unfounded or unnecessary criticism. One thing is sure: if someone can find grounds for criticizing writing, they will. So steal their thunder and, if you are asked, be able to name not only which variant you are using but also why.

Do try to be consistent in this, because consistency in approach underpins a strong, quality-conscious corporate image. You undermine this if some people in your company use UK English spellcheck and grammar check and others use US English versions. It happens all the time, often without people realizing. Active decisions are needed here.

This series gives you practical help to succeed in opening doors to international trade by means of your writing. I focus on the successful experiences of companies who have used the methods I show. These users are both native and non-native speakers of English. This is because both groups share common problems when writing English for business. This may perhaps surprise you, as will the fact that the same solutions can apply.

Just as the series is not about 'taking you back to school', it is not even necessarily about gaining the proficiency of a native English speaker. As you have seen, I have already hinted that not all native speakers are proficient! Instead, the series is all about reaching the level of competence you need in order to succeed in everything you write. The objective is that you never need to feel insecure again. Quite the reverse: you will feel confident, simply by knowing what to do and how to do it. A large part of this new-found confidence will come from understanding how simply expressed facts are understood best and impress the most, even with complex subject matter.

The whole series reinforces messages (a proven way to help you learn) and uses a building-block approach. So if a topic is introduced in one book of the series, it may be approached from a different angle in another. It really is as simple as that. All you need is a systematic approach and willingness to succeed. If you are ready, let's go!

Defining native and non-native English speakers

For ease of reference, when I refer to native English speakers I mean anyone who speaks any variety of English as their first language.

The ways in which non-native English speakers learn English can be categorized broadly as: English as an acquired language (EAL), English as a foreign language (EFL), English for speakers of other languages (ESOL), all of which are self-explanatory, and English as a second language (ESL). In the ESL category, learners are likely to be in a setting where the main or official language is English but their native tongue is not. It can be a confusing term when used to describe someone who is actually learning English as a third or fourth language, as can be the case.

There is some debate within academic circles as to which expression (or others) should be used. As this is not an academic but business-oriented book, I choose to use a different convention here. So throughout this book you will find that I use:

- ■ the term native English (NE) speaker or writer to denote a person whose first language is English, and native English (NE) writing to refer to their writing;

- ■ the term non-native English (non-NE) speaker or writer to denote a person whose first language is not English, and non-native English (non-NE) writing to refer to their writing.

Common problems with English for global business

The fact that English is used so extensively for global business yields quite a surprising result. It means that written business English will ultimately be directed more at a non-native English (non-NE) audience than at a native English audience. As well as there being different varieties of English, there are, in effect, sub-varieties directly caused by mixing English with the language patterns of the native country. Examples are Chinglish (Chinese-English), Manglish (Malaysian-English) and Singlish (Singapore-English). The same phenomenon can happen in any language mix.

Sometimes this can lead to out-and-out mistranslations and although users may understand what they mean, these can be unintelligible to the foreign reader. Indeed, to take Chinglish as an example, during the planning stage for the 2008 Beijing Olympics, the Chinese authorities saw a need to try to root out the problem that they realized existed. Anticipating a huge influx of foreign visitors, they realized that mistranslations appeared in the public places where visitors would go: on menus in restaurants and on road signs, and also in writing connected with exporting, including labels on products. As one municipal spokesman acknowledged, 'the misinformation had become a headache for foreigners', so they asked people to help them address the problem and unearthed examples such as:

'To take notice of safe, the slippery are very crafty' = Warning: slippery path.

In a gym: 'The treadmill is in the middle of repairing' = The treadmill is being repaired.

In another assessment, the Singapore government has discouraged the use of Singlish in favour of Singapore Standard English. Though many feel that Singlish is a valid marker of Singaporean identity, the government believes that a standard English improves Singaporeans' ability to communicate effectively with other English users throughout the world.

So problems can arise when we take a global perspective. Even if I just look at a sample of anglicized words used in Western Europe, similar problems can be apparent. I see expressions such as 'a parking' (UK English: a car park; US English: a parking lot) or 'presentation charts' used predominantly in Germany (UK English and US English: presentation slides) or 'handy' in continental Europe (UK English: mobile phone; US English: cellphone) or 'beamer' in France and elsewhere (UK English: projector). But if we are writing globally, by definition we have to realize that we are not just writing for readers in one country.

Let's look again at that word 'charts' used by many German companies for presentation slides. To a native English reader, the word refers to graphs or tables. If someone says they are preparing some charts to include in their presentation and then e-mails over some slides without any graphs or tables, what am I am likely to assume? That the presentation is complete or incomplete? It will probably be the latter – and valuable time may be lost before I e-mail or telephone that person to ask when I am going to receive the 'missing' items. So here is an instance where quirky use of English can slow down business results simply because it attempts to redefine a standard meaning – and confuses the wider, global audience.

Let's also look again at the words 'handy' for mobile phone or 'beamer' for projector. In these cases, the vast majority of native English speakers are unlikely to have any idea what these words mean. You need to think about how the whole issue impacts on your company, as we will now see.

Define business English within your company

My suggestion is this. Carry out some sort of survey to evaluate whether the terms you are using really are understood by your target audience. Terms that are understood in Western

Europe may not have the same currency in Asian markets and so on. Just because English-sounding words and expressions have crept into your company usage, this does not mean they are internationally recognized.

Then share your findings throughout your company, to gain consensus on how to describe the business English you plan to use. If you have just started your career, you can impress your boss by doing this. You can make a difference, boost your prospects and help your organization shine.

One important point to note is that any variety of business English will be in state of flux. You will find more about this in Chapter 3.

Your checklist for action

Answer the following questions to help you decide what you could do better:

- Do you communicate with a specific group of English users? Or are you likely to be communicating worldwide?

- Do you identify and then use a single type of English every time you write in English? Or do you need to vary it according to your target audience each time?

- Do you set your computer spellcheck and grammar check to the type(s) of English you use?

- If so, do you check that it does not default to US English spelling (unless that is your preferred variety)?

- Do you regularly check that the words you use are understood by your readers?

- When you do not understand a word, do you feel confident enough to ask its meaning, in order both to understand it and give feedback to the writer?

3

Writing English for global business

Looking at how you use English at work

It is useful for you and your colleagues (where this applies) to hold up a figurative mirror, in order to evaluate as far as is possible:

- How your readers see themselves.

- How you see yourselves.

- How you see your readers.

- How your readers may see you through your writing.

It is amazing how the images may diverge, and successful writing will take this into account. Its aim will be to remove distortions, bringing the four equally important images together into sharp, correct focus. You cannot achieve this focus without appreciating and also embracing the fact that different cultures communicate differently. If you are dealing with a particular country, you will naturally want and need to carry out more detailed research as to the right way to communicate with their culture.

In outline, though, it is true to say that a typical North European style of writing comes over as structured and fairly direct. If we specifically look at a typical British style, there can be a tendency to waffle – even though people largely know that plain, simple English is preferable. Is it perhaps because English has such a rich vocabulary and a wealth of words is available to native speakers?

If we look at Asian cultures, we can find extremely polite, formal, self-effacing communication. It can be considered bad style to get to the point too quickly and rude to make points too directly. So these cultures are less likely to default to a structure considered normal by many: namely, main points, discussion of impact, then further information. Instead they are likely to have a stronger focus on introduction, setting a respectful tone, developing rapport, and then ending on the main points (which may be implied rather than enumerated).

Do take time to think about your cultural writing style and how you may need to adapt according to the cultures with which you do business.

Do your words say what you think they say?

You might be surprised to hear that major UK companies and government agencies call me in to be a troubleshooter to check over their English business writing for the UK market too. They ask me to look at the words they use (to internal and external customers, suppliers and so on) in order to help them evaluate whether these words really say what the companies want them to say. You see, using business English at work is not just about learning how to write words in English. It is as much about adopting the right frame of mind to be able to make the right connections with readers. You need to stand back and see your writing from all angles. The moment you say 'I did not mean that!' is the moment you realize that no, your writing does not add up as you intended. It is not saying the right things.

Throughout this series you will see that writing business English is about reducing verbosity, avoiding misunderstandings and crafting clear, concise messages. But the fewer words you write, the more important it is that you get them right.

Writing problems faced by non-native English writers

Everybody faces a very real challenge when communicating. This challenge is about how to succeed in conveying our precise meaning to those with whom we wish to communicate. We all have to work out how to convert what we are thinking into words. When we have to write, we face additional problems. Are these the right words to put down on paper, when we may not be there to explain them to readers?

There are so many factors that can distort our intended meanings, and this book will show you how to avoid many of them. This challenge can be far greater for non-native speakers of English. They have an extra step to overcome: to translate their words from their native language into English before they then write them down.

So if as a non-native English speaker you are to write effectively in English, it will be helpful for you to be systematic in approach. A sequence that should help you is this:

1. Identify the thought effectively in your own language.

2. Translate it correctly from your own language into English.

3. You may then need to convert the thought captured in English into the correct written English word.

4. Then make sure that the 'correct written English word' is actually the one that your readers can interpret correctly.

5. Having done all this, your English writing should enable readers to respond the way you want. And that is what you are in business for!

So let's work together to see how you can minimize any distortions. You don't want them interrupting this very important sequence. It's really important to get it right, from the planning stage through to delivery.

Use plain English when you can

When writing for global business, it is best to express the gist of what you are saying in really accessible, plain English. As I have just mentioned, do not focus on just translating from your own language into English. The more you do this, the worse things can get. Why? Because simply translating can result in:

- over-complicated or incorrect messages;

- focusing on the specific words rather than the overall meaning;

- losing sight of the normal business need to write a call to action.

So regularly ask yourself questions such as the following. Will my readers recognize the words I use? Will they understand their meaning? Am I enabling the response I need? Will my business achieve its desired goals as a result?

Problems with non-native English writing for native English speakers

The problems that can arise from non-native English (non-NE) writing do not affect only non-NE readers. Native English speakers and readers can be affected too. Let me list some of these effects:

- We cannot entirely understand the non-NE writer's writing.

- We cannot understand one or more aspects of the writing.

- We almost understand what is meant but do not ask questions as we should (either out of goodwill or because we cannot be bothered).

- This can lead to the wrong meaning continuing to be communicated, which can lead to all sorts of problems.

Reading a non-NE writer's approximation to a real English word can, over time, make the native reader begin to accept that word as correct. As an example, I have seen 'automisation' written by so many foreign companies over the years that I almost begin to accept it as real English, even though you will not find it in a dictionary. The trouble is, its inferred meaning is not as clear as it might seem. Native English speakers may assume it is used for 'automation', which can be the case. But very often non-NE writers use it to mean 'computerization'.

Other problems can be:

- Strangely enough (and wrongly, in my opinion), native English speakers can get defensive if their English is corrected by non-NE writers, who can have a very good grasp of English grammar.

- Native English writers and speakers can be unsure whether they should correct non-NE writers who make spelling or grammatical mistakes or whose meanings are unclear.

- Native English writers and speakers can be supremely irritated by one-word or one-line messages that some non-NE writers see as supremely efficient.

- Native English writers and speakers can be equally irritated by over-complicated non-NE writing that has unclear meanings and requires implied rather than stated action.

I give examples of these throughout this series of books.

Knowing that these reactions occur is instrumental in helping you understand not only how to write but also how to seek readers' feedback, to judge how well you are doing. If we are failing our readers, we need to re-design our writing. We need to know the problems first, in order that we can work on the solutions to get it right each time.

Problems posed for native and non-native English writers alike

Let's look at some features that can perplex both native English and non-NE writers alike.

Idioms, clichés and nuances

Idioms are expressions that are peculiar to a language, where simply by translating the words, non-natives may be unable to work out what their meanings are. It is true that you can feel great when you master some idioms in a foreign language. I feel like I am the 'bee's knees'; I am 'over the moon' about it. Do you get the drift of what I am saying, or am I pulling the wool over your eyes? Are you completely puzzled? You could reach for your dictionary but it will take you precious time, so let me explain:

- 'To be the bee's knees' means to be really good, to be excellent.

- 'Over the moon' means delighted.

- 'To get the drift' of something means to get the general meaning.

- 'To pull the wool over someone's eyes' means to deceive them or obscure something from them.

In actual fact, native speakers may also misunderstand idioms, particularly as some are quite obscure. Do approach them with caution in business. However competent you may feel in using them, the odds are they will lead to confusion and misunderstanding.

Let's consider clichés now. 'Cliché' has been imported from French into many languages, but, interestingly, it does not always mean the same thing in each. In German, for example, it means a stereotype, whereas in UK English it has a different meaning. It signifies a stale expression: something that has been overused to the point that it is ineffective. A cliché can even undermine a person's writing. Why should readers be impressed by writing that seems tired and boring?

Here are some examples of clichés, with their meanings shown in brackets:

'In this day and age' (now);

'It will fall on deaf ears' (it will be ignored);

'Not to put too fine a point on it' (this means).

'Nuance' is another word that English has imported from French. It means shade or subtlety in language. Unsurprisingly, even native writers can have difficulty understanding nuances. As an example, in one online discussion forum I noticed some English-speaking artists engaged in debate. They were questioning what the differences were between the words tint, hue, shade and so on, when describing aspects of colour. There were many conflicting suggestions and very little consensus. So nuances can be tricky things.

In a business context, let's look at how the subtlety in meaning between 'quite proud' and 'proud' can actually lead to problems. First of all, are you aware that there is a difference in meaning? To a British speaker 'proud' usually has a stronger emphasis than 'quite proud'. If I tell someone I am proud of their work achievements, it's an absolute. They have done very well and I'm telling them that. The moment I say that I am 'quite proud', the perception can be that I'm diluting my pride: I am less proud than I could be. The nuance then implies that the person could have done better.

But very confusingly, I have heard an American boss tell a member of staff that he was 'quite proud' of his achievements. I could hear his intonation in the spoken words. This distinctly told me that he was using 'quite proud' to mean 'very proud'. But we cannot hear intonation in writing (except when we SHOUT through capital letters). So if we use nuances whereby the words persist in meaning different things to different people, these words will not ultimately make commercial sense. So if you can avoid nuances, then why not make life easier, and matters clearer, by doing so?

Standard and online dictionaries; and the lure of cut and paste

Everyone should check the meanings and spellings of words when unsure. And, whatever you do, do not feel you have to use the most complicated word that your dictionary may offer.

Let's say you are a non-NE writer, you are online and you type a word in your own language for 'outcome'. You click on the dictionary for a selection of English translation words. I tried this in German once and the online dictionary offered, amongst other words: corollary and consecution. Corollary is a word that people may know but would use only in a very specific context. Consecution, though? That is definitely online dictionary-speak.

Non-NE writers can wrongly feel they must choose the most complicated 'intelligent-sounding' choice – which is often the longest – when they come face to face with a bewildering selection of words to choose from. So out goes 'outcome', that almost everyone will understand, and in comes 'consecution'. Is it really an 'intelligent choice' if your readers do not know what you mean?

So we can see how just one wrong word can cause chaos with your meaning. But online dictionaries also ensnare users to use whole phrases where one word would suffice. 'Wow,' you may say. 'This is easy, isn't it? And it looks good!' But it will not look good if you have not taken context into account – and a very possible need to adjust your grammar. Some phrases are so specific that if you put them in the wrong place (and this can be a danger with 'cut and paste') your writing becomes gibberish: nonsense, in short.

I keyed the word 'profits' into one online dictionary and was really amused when it suggested I could use a related phrase: 'the profits of doom'! All right, there may be a global recession, but this is ridiculous. The reference should have been 'prophets of doom', which means people who predict the future and identify hazards ahead. If I were a non-NE writer, I could easily have accepted that this expression exists. Might I not look silly otherwise? I might be seen as not belonging to the club of seasoned professionals who reel off the latest English buzz words. Why put 'my head above the parapet' in order to be 'shot down'?

I think it is rather like the story of the Emperor's new clothes. Someone has to stand up and say 'That's not right!' And it does take self-confidence to do this, which I hope this book will give you in abundance. So if you can, do look for the word that is in common usage (that is, the word that people really use). Do not be disappointed if this is likely to be more prosaic than the language of Shakespeare. You write intelligently in English for business when your readers understand you.

Business writing as communication

There are two main routes whereby we transmit a series of thoughts from our brains to other people's brains. These are speech and writing. Each transmission can be broken down into a sequence of steps, each of which carries an associate risk of distortion.

Here is a very clear example of a distorted message:

> Identifying business writing has to be about messages. Present them you should then in a key that will engage readers' attention – and make them want way to read more.

How did you react to this piece of writing? Did you try to make any sense of it? Did you manage to decode it? Because that is what you would have had to do. And often we find ourselves reading writing that, although not as jumbled as this example, is not far off.

Here is the decoded message:

> Business writing has to be about identifying key messages. You should then present them in a way that will engage readers' attention – and make them want to read more.

You can see how distortion makes a mockery of good advice. So let's now work on identifying the differing ways business readers can react to muddled messages. Write down any ideas of your own. My findings include these:

- The readers might not be bothered to work out the meaning. Unimpressed, they might walk away from the 'message' – and from the business that it belongs to.

- Such readers might also tell others the bad news.

- Readers might try to work out a meaning: they might decipher it wrongly and do nothing.

- Or they might take the wrong action.

- Readers cannot understand and they need to ask for clarification.

- Readers might be offended and not tell you.

- Readers might complain to you.

Can you see the commercial implications involved in these scenarios? Let's list them here:

- Inaction from readers, or their failure to react the desired way, is bad news.

- Lost custom and goodwill speak for themselves and affect your profits.

- A bad reputation (spread by unhappy readers telling others) can undermine your success and damage your business.

- Being on the receiving end of wrong action is clearly appalling for any business.

- Clarifying messages involves doing the same job twice or more.

- Insulting readers is never going to be good for any business.

- Complaints may be good news in one sense (you get to hear what your customer thinks, and you can change) but they are also bad news – and they cost you.

English continues to evolve

I mentioned in Chapter 1 how business writing is in a state of flux and how writing in English also continues to change. Indeed, modern English has evolved from so many influences: most words in English are of Anglo-Saxon origin (linked to the language spoken by tribes from Denmark and northern Germany who settled in England in the fifth and sixth centuries). Many other words originate from Latin, Greek, French, Celtic and Dutch; others have been adopted from a colonial past. The list goes on. It makes the English very proud of their extremely rich vocabulary, even though they may not have the 22 words for different types of snow that the Eskimos apparently have!

The English used in business today can seem surprisingly informal to many. In France there is an academy dedicated to 'upholding standards' in the way the French language is used. One of its objectives is to keep the language as uncorrupted by outside influences as possible. There is no such English equivalent. However, there is ongoing debate between factions, which I will summarize very broadly. On one side are those who believe in prescribing rules of traditional grammar etc. On the other are those who believe it is more about examining how language evolves and which usages prevail.

That is why you may be puzzled when some English teachers tell you that you can, for example, write 'to boldly go' – thereby splitting the infinitive form of the verb 'to go'. (Some will even dispute whether there is such a thing as an infinitive form in English, as it is not a Latinate language.) More traditional, prescriptive teachers will take a contrary view. They are likely to say you can never split the infinitive, so you would have to write 'to go boldly'.

You will also find that feelings can run strongly regarding which of the following is correct:

Understand who are you writing for.

Understand for whom you are writing.

Most people will accept either version (and looking at modern business writing, most would probably write the first), though the prescriptive school will opt for the second. This would be on the basis that (i) 'who' can only be the subject of the sentence (and it isn't here) and (ii) you cannot end a sentence with 'for', as it is a preposition.

So what can you do in view of this dilemma? The advice I constantly give is: reflect the expectations of your target readership. One size will not fit all. Because both English and business writing itself are in a state of flux, sometimes you will find that a middle course is the route to success. Each chapter in this book contains many practical tips to help you.

An advantage you can have as a non-native English writer

The most forward-thinking, successful companies where English is not the first language often actively encourage and train employees to perfect the English writing skills they need. In a positive learning culture such as this, great importance can also be attached to customers' perception of quality and professionalism. Ironically, it can result in non-NE staff making more effort than native speakers in avoiding confusion and misunderstandings.

The very fact that you are reading this book suggests that, far from being daunted and overwhelmed by the task in hand, you have a winning attitude. You are seeking solutions.

How complacency can disadvantage native writers

Native speakers of any language can assume they are proficient in their own language, so 'of course people understand what we say and write'. But it is not necessarily true. Every company should really assess writing ability when recruiting and/or promoting employees into jobs that need this skill. Otherwise complacency sets in – and complacency drains the lifeblood of any organization. It is how companies lose the competitive edge.

So let me show you some practical examples where native English writers got it wrong and paid the price.

An upmarket hotel opened its new restaurant, meant to be called *The Brasserie*. Unfortunately, nobody checked the correct spelling of this French word. The restaurant opened to great fanfare. The trouble was, it was called *The Brassiere*. It was not long before it was ridiculed in the national press – but it was long enough for it to lose face (and money on the signage, menus and advertising, all of which had to be redone).

Another unfortunate piece of writing by a native English speaker was this: 'I feel I have become a prawn in the game.' He actually meant to write 'pawn in the game' (using a chess analogy) but the extra letter made a nonsense of this.

So you see it is not just foreigners who make mistakes. But the uplifting fact is that, whatever the nationality, it is virtually always the good who strive to be better!

Your checklist for action

To use business English at work, your words and the framework that surround them have to be perfect. This is achievable, so why set the bar lower? Maybe it will help to list the stark consequences of getting it wrong:

> Business writing mistakes (including unclear, confusing or alienating messages) can equal lost cash + lost custom + lost goodwill.

For these reasons:

- Make sure that your message is not subordinate to your translation.

- You may be unable to explain things as precisely as you would like, so may have to focus on the main messages that are essential for readers to know (except for contracts, technical documents etc, where every detail matters!).

■   Make sure that you get your message right for your recipient: more complicated text can be counterproductive and confusing for you and your reader.

■   If you are preoccupied with correctly describing what you do, you can lose sight of the bigger picture (eg the need to express how you do it better than the rest, to win and retain custom).

■   Do the work for your readers: make sure your messages are not losing you (or them) time or money.

■   No matter how good our English language skills are, we all need to take the time to check our written English.

4

Business writing for today

Winning business through English

Years ago, it often took longer to do deals than it does today. The ritual involved in the initial telephone enquiries or formal letters of introduction, preliminary and follow-up meetings and the like could almost mask the true point of why two or more parties were 'sounding each other out'.

Incidentally, did you notice the deliberately long-winded style of that last sentence? It mimics how writing in English used to be, when life was perhaps less pressured. Business writing develops as language changes, and it continues to evolve in other ways too. There are cultural differences that I have mentioned. In addition, the layer of detailed introductions and small talk has partly given way to addressing the real purpose: to drive business success.

Once again there may be a gap between how you were taught to write English at school and how you need to write it for business. English for business today is very much about 'how to win business through English'.

Academic writing compared with writing for business

These are two almost entirely different genres. The goals are different and they require different approaches, which I will outline now.

Academic writing requirements

Students are generally required to write structured essays, research papers and theses. These are largely marked on the basis of how well students have managed to access the right information, process this, show prose-composition skills and accuracy, and conform to a fairly standard presentation format. By and large, the structure involves a beginning (topic and purpose), a middle (evidence and argument, or thesis) and an end (conclusion). The words and tone used must be relevant for the world of academe. This can often require a formal, passive style (objectivity rather than subjectivity); an extensive, specialized vocabulary can gain marks.

Business writing requirements

In the workplace, you certainly need to know how to access the right information and process this when you write. You need to be accurate too. Some companies require you to follow a standard house style. However, even then you may be allowed to make suggestions about how the house style could evolve, in view of changing business circumstances and customers' needs.

But here is one very interesting recent evolution in writing business English. There are definitely fewer occasions now when business writing is seen to have the academic-style beginning, middle and end structure (other than in certain formal reports). You will find that you need to develop new literacy skills that your teachers may not have taught you and that you may not have come across previously. This can present a dilemma to businesses, as I will now show you.

You can use 'I' when you write in business

People may need to shed the shackles of school-driven writing when they enter the workplace. For example, time after time I hear people say, 'We were taught at school that we cannot use "I" and "we" in the same sentence in a letter,' or 'You cannot write "I" in business; it must always be "we".' People can go for years unable to free themselves from this constraint.

Many companies feel that a key driver of business success is empowerment of the individual. It is about everyone being given the power and encouragement to make a difference within their organization. There may be 'no I in team' (I am using this management-speak ironically here!) but to embrace the concept of 'I/me' is surely crucial. Surely we have to be allowed to write 'I'. Surely we should also be allowed to write 'we' (even within the same piece of writing), to demonstrate that each of us is an integral part of the total company. You will certainly find plenty of evidence from companies worldwide that yes, you can indeed use 'I' and 'we' within your sentences.

Other things that you may wish to 'unlearn'

You may have been taught that you cannot begin a sentence with 'And' or 'But'. Actually you can – and many acclaimed writers do. For traditionalists, let me mention the famous English novelist Jane Austen as one example. I often begin sentences with these words throughout this series, as the style seems relevant for today. This is largely because e-mail is today's predominant business writing and globally people write for it in a style that is halfway between conversation and formal writing. What's more, it is having a noticeable effect on the way people write other documentation. This is not about 'dumbing down'; it is about expressing facts simply, in accessible writing that speaks to people.

Now it is true to say that if I had a specific customer or line manager who hated sentences beginning with 'And' or 'But', I would not use that style with them. Similarly, if my publishers did not accept the style, I would also avoid it – but they agree it is appropriate for standard business English writing. Naturally, it is essential to be reader-driven when you write. As I cannot have the advantage of knowing each of you, my readers, I will have to use a generic style.

If you believe in being practical, you could keep a list of expressions you know some people do not like. It can become almost immaterial whether these expressions are strictly correct or not, if our readers have an aversion to them. There are always alternatives you can choose that are less likely to lead you into controversy. Here are some examples that regularly crop up in my training workshops. Where at all possible, people prefer to read:

'For this to work, you/we need to...' rather than 'It must be done.'

'Yes, I've done that' rather than 'Done.'

'Thank you for bringing this to our attention' rather than 'We note...'

'So that we can reach our targets, please could I have these figures tomorrow?' rather than 'I need these figures tomorrow.'

'We regret we are unable to help' rather than 'We cannot help.'

Can you see the pattern that is emerging? People tend not to like terseness and they like to be given reasons why things have to be done. If you expressly ask for their assistance, their help is more likely to be forthcoming.

Listen to readers' feedback

It is a very good idea to ask readers for feedback on your business English writing. We can learn so much from this. Companies who take the time to do so find that readers routinely comment that:

- They feel patronized by poorly written letters.

- They can feel insulted by writers' lack of attention to the right detail.

- They don't sense the 'human touch' in much of the language used in business writing.

- They can feel so angered by correspondence that, where they can do so, they will walk away from the business concerned.

- They dislike excessive use of jargon (words or expressions used by a particular profession or group that are sometimes unnecessarily difficult – and certainly difficult for others to understand), over-complicated sentences and confusing use of words.

■   They are offended when their personal details are written incorrectly.

I suggest that you reread this list from time to time. Never lose sight of how readers may react. I will be dealing with all these aspects of writing in this book but will just highlight one of them now, as it is one of the most common. It is this: what do you think the lack of the 'human touch' in writing could mean? Is it the fact that business writers actively avoid using 'people' words such as 'you' and 'we'? Failing to use people words often happened in the past and, unfortunately, it can still be seen today. Let me demonstrate. A company writes to a client on the following lines:

Dear Sir

Re: Policy XYZ

It has come to the company's attention that the aforementioned policy that is about to expire has not yet been renewed. I enclose a renewal form, which you need to return within seven days, otherwise you will no longer be afforded cover.

Yours faithfully
John Smith

Smith and Co

Some companies still use stilted, old-fashioned English to write this way and I cannot imagine why. Especially not now, as we live in a world where customers increasingly expect to feel valued. So how can this depersonalized approach make the client feel valued? I will redesign the message, using people words and more modern English.

Dear (client's name)

Invitation to renew your policy

We would like to invite you to renew your policy, which is shortly due to expire on (date) and would like to ensure that you continue to have the cover you need.

So please could you read, then complete as necessary, the enclosed renewal form, and return it to us by (date)?

If you have any further queries in relation to this letter, please do not hesitate to contact me on (telephone number and/or e-mail address).

With thanks.
Yours sincerely
John Smith

Smith and Co

Choosing the right style

More examples follow, showing how writers and readers alike can be confused when faced with differing styles of written English within their own company.

1. Therefore, although obviously we cannot make any assessment about the matter in hand on this occasion, we will nevertheless take cognizance of the contents of your letter and will forthwith forward a copy thereof to the managing director who has the appropriate responsibility for investigating any issues raised.

2. Done.

3. Thanks loads ☺.

The style in the first example is extremely formal English and quite old-fashioned in feel. You can see what I term barrier words: 'therefore', 'obviously', 'nevertheless' and 'forthwith'. They are all correct English, but they can make readers feel distanced. The majority of readers will probably view the writer as condescending towards an 'inferior' reader, rather than communicating with a valued customer.

The one word 'Done' in the second example is a common e-mail response these days, when someone has asked a question such as 'Have you completed this action?' Those who write the one-word reply usually feel they are very effective workers and communicators. What they do not see is the irritation that the one-word e-mail reply can cause. It is so often seen as discourteous. Just by adding three words and changing the reply to 'I have done that' can improve readers' perception. The writing becomes less curt and more polite. As people comment on this in so many training workshops that I run, it is well worth a mention here.

The third example is informal in the extreme, yet you will see it a lot in business today. It does convey goodwill. But many will find it unprofessional and do not feel it is appropriate for corporate communication. Some writers may argue that they are only that informal when writing for a known internal recipient. But the problem is, e-mails can so often continue in threads – and may be forwarded in time to external recipients too.

In short, you are quite likely to see these contrasts in business English writing in your company. Do consider whether taking a middle course, a median between an overly formal or overly informal style, is going to work best, to avoid unnecessarily confusing styles – and even offence.

Ideal communication

It is hard to define ideal business communication but this summary may help:

> Effective written communication is when the correct, concise, current message is sent out to the primary receiver(s), then onwards without distortion to further receivers to generate the required response.

Let me amplify what I mean. Sometimes we write to someone simply to inform them of something. They may not need to do anything other than note what we have said. They then remain the primary receiver. The only response we require is one that favours the way we have delivered the message (both on a personal and a company level).

Probably more often our aim when we write is to do more than simply inform. We are looking for the receiver(s) to respond not just favourably to our style but to act in response, in the way and at the time we desire. Our writing should actively enable this through the formula we design. So it is crucial that it can be understood by all who read it (directly or indirectly), in order to achieve our objectives and cover our readers' needs.

Why have I included the word 'current' in the formula? This is because so often people systematically address the first three points I list, but then forget to update the information. So the best-laid plans can get messed up.

Here is an example. An external trainer is going to deliver a course for 10 members of a company's staff. One week earlier, their manager issues joining instructions to all attending. The course is scheduled to be held in the Byfield Room in a hotel the company uses. The trainer has been sent the full list of names and has asked the company to notify any changes before the day.

By the day of the training no changes have been communicated and the trainer arrives for set-up. He finds that the hotel has changed the venue to the Smithson Room, which has not been laid out as requested. There are no flipcharts and no projector screen.

By the 9 am start of the course only seven attendees turn up. The trainer calls the company to check but the relevant manager is not available. So the trainer puts back the start time, in case the missing delegates are held up in traffic. He later finds out that the company were aware that three delegates would be unable to attend on the day.

Can you see why the failures to relay changes cost money and impede performance? Both the hotel and the client company were at fault here. Although the course went ahead, there was unnecessary hassle and a distinct lack of professionalism. It also made for a chaotic scene which is likely to undermine delegates' perception of the day in total. This kind of thing happens all too frequently. It comes as a direct result of people not reading and responding, not making calls or writing e-mails to update and inform others of changing or changed circumstances. A minor series of events can turn a well-organized programme into an unprofessional shambles.

The Word Power Skills system: four easy steps to success

This series of books is here to guide and help you succeed in every aspect of writing English for business, from the simplest to the most complex tasks you will have to deal with. The system I now introduce appears in each book in the series.

A guide to premier business writing

The system uses the idea of 'a ladder of success', in which you start at the bottom (Step 1) and systematically climb to success (beyond Step 4) as follows:

Step 1

Be correct:

- Know what your writing needs to achieve, alongside what your company needs to achieve.

- At the very least, match readers' minimum expectations.

- Ensure that your writing is free of mistakes.

Your business communication will fail if you get your basics wrong.

Step 2

Be clear:

- Use plain English and express facts as simply as possible.

- Edit so that your main points are easily understood.

Confused messages undermine your objectives. They can lose you custom too.

Step 3

Make the right impact:

- Use the right words and layout to get noticed for the right reasons.

- Use the right style to present yourself and your company well.

- Create opportunities.

The right impact differentiates you from competitors and helps bring about the responses you need.

Step 4

Focus on readers as your customers:

- Write from their perspective.

- Empathize with them.

- Favour positive, proactive words.

- Avoid words that put up barriers, and avoid jargon wherever you can.

Use your written words to satisfy and, if possible, delight your customers.

Your checklist for action

- Be aware that your readers and customers are likely to have a negative impression of (or reject) ineffective writing.

- Evaluate feedback on your own specific business English writing. You can do this simply by checking your answers to questions such as the following:

  - When you send a memo, do people often not bother to read it?

- Do you have to send out the same message more than once?

- Do people ever congratulate you or complain about the tone of your message?

- Are your letters, reports or e-mails significantly longer than those of your colleagues?

- When you receive new details, do you always update people who need to know?

▪ Bear in mind that there are differences between academic English writing and business English writing.

▪ Be aware that academic writing often has a formal structure and objective slant. Business writing is tending to become more informal, especially because of the rise in e-mail and web writing, where material is presented in bite-sized chunks.

▪ Be prepared to unlearn some of the rules you may have learnt at school.

5

Quality matters

Why it really matters to get your writing right

You need to get your business English writing right, first time and every time. Contribute to your own success by understanding that each bit of business writing you send out can be (indeed, should be) viewed as a personal as well as a company advertisement. Written words are 'frozen' in the point of time in which they were written. They are likely to be judged for what they are, when we may not be there to explain them.

To succeed they have to be the right words for our commercial purpose at the time, or we will fall at the first hurdle. Yet they also have to be right from our readers' point of view, or we will fall at the second hurdle.

To make mistakes is only human?

The trouble is that whoever we are, whatever we do and whatever our proficiency in a language, we are likely to make mistakes in our writing. In fact, we are likely to make the occasional mistake in most aspects of our business performance, even when we know our subject matter very well. Why? Well, ironically, we can be lulled into a false sense of security. We can expect our writing to be right – though we often achieve better results when we expect it to be wrong. This is because, when we think our writing might be wrong, we are more likely to:

■ identify mistakes;

■ eradicate them before we send our writing out;

■ as a result of these factors, present a totally professional corporate image.

Checking, and even double-checking, your writing before you send it can pay great dividends. It may mean you spend longer than you would like at the planning stage but this is well worthwhile. It raises the odds that each message you send out is right.

How readers can react to written mistakes

Just take a look at three sentences written by non-native English writers. I will identify the problems in each case and explain for each how readers might react.

1.   Thank you for your order. You are demanded to send payment within 30 days.

First of all, the expression 'you are demanded' is not correct English. It would be better to write something on the lines of 'Please send payment within 30 days' or 'You are requested to pay within 30 days.' In English there is an expression 'to demand payment' but it has a very strong connotation. It is generally used to denote the final notice before a company pursues legal action, to collect money owing to it in an overdue account. When the expression is used validly, it would be on the following lines:

This is a final demand for payment (within 30 days) of your outstanding account.

So in our first example we have an outright grammatical mistake. But the wrong tone can also count as a writing mistake. Let's look at the text again: 'Thank you for your order. You are demanded to send payment within 30 days.' Although the reader sees the initial words 'Thank you,' the next sentence introduces a harsh, accusatory tone. Yet this is clearly one of the first points of contact between customer and company. The order has just been placed: 'Thank you for your order' tells us that. So is the customer going to feel that this is a nice company to do business with? I do not think so.

Let's not forget that, in business, we should try to ensure that when new customers place their orders, we make this a very positive experience for them. If a company cannot be bothered to write well here, then the indicators are not good for future business success. Customers usually have a choice: there is likely to be an alternative company that is nice to do business with.

2.   We can provide the services you outline in principal but
     we request a supplementation.

Homonyms are words that have the same sound and sometimes the same spelling as another but whose meanings are
different. They can confuse native English and non-NE writers
alike. You will find more on homonyms in Chapter 8. But
let's just take a look here at two words that are frequently
confused. They are:

Principal: an adjective generally meaning first in importance;
also a noun meaning a chief or senior person; can also mean
an original sum of money for investment.

Principle: a noun meaning a fundamental truth or quality; a
rule or belief governing a person's morally correct behaviour
and attitudes.

If we go back to our second example, unfortunately the
writer has chosen the wrong version of the homonym here.
The correct word would be 'principle'. Some readers may
not mind this; some will not notice. But some will make a
value judgement: this is wrong. It may be unfair but just one
wrong word can undermine readers' perception of a writer's
or a company's professionalism. It can also distract readers'
attention away from the writer's key message.

Moving along the sentence in our second example, we find
another confusing word. A 'supplementation'? What does this
mean? Is it a request for further information? Is it a request
for a supplementary fee, that is to say, more money? Or is it a
deposit (part pre-payment)? Once again, it is the sort of word
that an online dictionary search would suggest and one which
a native English writer would not use! Their writing would
'ask for more details or further information'.

A crucial point is this: writing English for business really
should not be about 'over-Englishing the English', as I call it.

This describes a compelling need that many non-native English writers feel. It is the mistaken belief that they must choose the most complicated vocabulary in any list they see. In today's pressured business environment, readers actually prefer it when facts are expressed simply. You can also get your message across faster and reduce the chance of misunderstandings.

3. You should benefit us of further informations as we feel ourselves unable to help you.

This sentence contains some very common mistakes made by non-NE writers. 'You should benefit us' is a construction that simply does not exist in standard English. Nor does 'inform-ations'. 'Information' exists only in the singular, no matter how much information is given (and incidentally, the same applies to 'training,' though I often see 'trainings'). The second verb phrase, 'we feel ourselves', uses the reflexive form that English uses far less frequently than many other languages. When English does use it, it tends to be in a very physical, literal sense. Here it would mean 'we are actually touching ourselves'. It does not imply the state of mind that the writer assumes it means – and the sentence simply does not sound right.

How might the reader react to these mistakes? Well, on the first level, grammatical mistakes do not impress. On a second level, the writer sounds unhelpful: once again the inference is that this is not a company that is nice – or indeed easy – to do business with. And when we use the very powerful word 'benefit' in business when we communicate with customers, it must be directed at them, not us. So the writer has potentially made a big mistake here from the reader's perspective. In some ways, I think this has happened because the writer has focused on translation, over and above the business purpose that should be central.

If we rewrite the sentence as: 'Please could you let us have some further information so that we can help you?' then this helps get the message back on track. It is simpler and it works.

Although I have just highlighted some mistakes, I do not advocate that you take a 'red pen' approach. This can be the approach some managers take, when they use a red pen and highlight an employee's written mistakes, in a clearly unsupportive way. This approach really can demotivate staff and is best avoided.

It is true that sometimes you just have to write the way your line managers suggest. But it is always better to know the reasons why they consider one way better than another. Even in UK English you can opt to write certain words in two ways, both of which are correct. I mentioned earlier that you can write 'recognize' or 'recognise', or 'judgement' or 'judgment' – and it can be personal or company preference that dictates which you use. If you do not understand the reasons why you must write a certain way, your manager owes it to you to explain why. But you also owe it to yourself to ask why.

It is in your own interests to know if you are making mistakes. Readers will see mistakes and they may comment on them. In business you can never afford 'to bury your head in the sand' – in other words, just because you do not acknowledge something, that does not mean it does not exist. Problems do occur and every business needs to identify them. How else can we seek solutions and get things right?

It is true that to make mistakes is human, but routinely making mistakes will never make good commercial sense. We do need to focus on quality, and it is a good idea to define what we mean by this. Does it mean top quality or simply acceptable? It is really up to each business to define what they expect the quality of their output to be. Alongside this, each business should also quantify the quality that customers expect of it. This lines up with one aspect of Step 1 on the ladder of success, which I described in the previous chapter.

Further costs of getting your writing wrong

We saw how things can go wrong when we do not update our written messages in the light of changed circumstances. The following scenario also shows the cost businesses can pay for getting writing wrong.

I submitted a database entry on my business to a company that was to include it in a Europe-wide guide. Their fee seemed reasonable, given the likely exposure to new business. I had to follow a restricted format and limited word count, so my entry was as follows:

TQI Word Power Skills Training

Activity: A UK company that provides business support services for every type of business. It provides business English services to help with marketing literature and communication skills training.

Services include editing, text correction or fine tuning, quality assurance, proof-reading, group workshops, individual coaching in business English and cross-cultural briefing.

These innovative, fully confidential business services are designed to help you assure the quality of your service or product and help you hit your commercial target first and every time.

TQI Word Power Skills training offers businesses of all types and sizes expert and affordable solutions for their business English needs, together with international experience from previous consultancy in the Netherlands.

Co-operation request: TQI Word Power Skills Training seeks companies requiring these services.

A few weeks later I received an invoice from the company in charge of the database. Attached to this was a copy of the entry as it had actually appeared. Unknown to me, the copy had already gone live, Europe-wide, one month before I received the invoice. The entry was now the one shown below. It includes a number of errors, made when the company inputted my original wording onto the database. Can you spot these mistakes?

TQI Word Power Skills training

Activity: UK company that provides business support services for every type of business, it provides Business english services to help with marketing literature and communication skills training.

Services include editing, text correction or fine tuning, quality assurance, proof reading, group workshops, infividual coaching in Business English and inter cultural breifing.

These Innovative fully confidential business services are designed to help you assure the quality of your service or product and help you hit your commercial target first and every time.

TQI Word Power Skills training offers businesses of all types and sizes expert and affordable solutions for their business English needs, international expereince from previous consultancy in the Netherland.

Co-operation request: TQI Word Power Skills Training seeks companies that require there servces.

Quite understandably, I was not at all happy, especially when I was presented with an invoice to pay for this appalling entry. Can you see why this would be? If you look closely, you will see that there is at least one mistake in each paragraph. Some are spelling mistakes, such as 'infividual' for 'individual, 'breifing' for 'briefing' and 'expereince' for 'experience'. Some are inconsistencies, such as business English and Business English. Both may be used, but it is better style to keep to a single use, certainly within one paragraph. The word innovative suddenly has a capital 'I', thus we find 'Innovative' even though the word is mid-sentence. And so on – the list goes on. One thing is sure: nobody ran a spellcheck or grammar check.

What ultimately was the cost of this regrettable incident? The answer is that there was a cost to pay on a number of different levels. I refused to pay the invoice because the entry was incorrect, so the company suffered the loss of that income. That company then had to redraft a correct entry, and replace the incorrect entry at their own cost. The cost to my company was in terms of undermined professional credibility (both in the short and long term).

You can easily see how such an apparently low-key set of mistakes can have a disastrous effect on the professional credibility of a company that is operating internationally.

In the final analysis, although the mistakes were not mine, they appeared to be mine. It was my company name and my details that appeared ... which leads me to the next section.

You can never fully outsource your writing

This is a topic that merits a lot of discussion, as it crops up so much in business. The point I am going to make here is that we need to analyse mistakes, learn from them and try to prevent the same errors happening again.

What the episode in the last section taught me was this: not to assume that because the version I sent for publishing was correct, the published version would be correct too. I was unaware that the advertising company used Apple Macs. This meant that they did not just cut and paste my Word document: they had to retype the copy themselves. Whether or not this was the case, I should have asked to see the final proof before publication. Printers often provide this as a matter of course, to cover themselves against complaints at a later stage. But note that word 'often'… it is not the same as 'always'!

If you outsource something and it goes wrong, the backlash becomes yours. You cannot outsource responsibility!

Checking for mistakes

It actually helps you to expect there will be mistakes in your writing draft. Here is an analogy. When I was learning to drive, my teacher gave me invaluable advice. I was told to imagine everyone on the road was a maniac. That way, he explained, I would always be alert to the fact that mistakes inevitably happen. What is more, I would be a better driver as a result. Far from being complacent, I would be more likely to respond quickly to ever-changing situations and take corrective action. Can you see how easily the advice applies to checking for mistakes in your English writing too?

Proofreading tips

Check everything you write before you send it out. Choose the ways that will help you from the following tips:

- Allow sufficient time for your proofreading. If you rush you may still overlook the mistakes you are looking for.

- It can be easier to proofread on paper than on a computer screen.

- Use a dictionary or grammar book to help you, or your computer's spelling and grammar check (set on the correct variant of English for your target audience). Do be aware that this is not fail-safe. It may let the wrong word(s) through, especially homophones (words which sound the same, although the meanings and spellings can be different) for example 'brake' for 'break', 'there' for 'their' and so on.

- Try reading your lines backwards (people sometimes use a ruler to read one line at a time a time, to avoid distraction). You do not check for meaning this way, you just check that the words are written correctly.

- Check for meaning and logical arrangement.

- Make a self-help list of any words that you regularly get wrong, so that you can check them quickly and effectively next time you write them.

Your checklist for action

- Understand that mistakes can and do happen.

- Make sure that you take steps to minimize this, such as running spellcheck and grammar check in the right variety of English.

- Understand that mistakes in your English are not just about spelling and grammar.

- They can also be when words are left out, when sentences confuse or present facts in a disorderly way that distorts the correct message.

- Understand the longer-term impact mistakes may have (and how these can in turn impact on you and your company).

- Highlight to others the importance of correct English writing.

- Always check your writing before you issue it.

- If you are not sure, ask for help from someone who will know.

6

Punctuation and grammar tips

Why punctuation and grammar matter

This extract shows what unpunctuated writing looks like:

mr jones the companys hr director called mrs smith into his office for an update on the latest recruitment drive he wanted to know whether the online application system was working reports had filtered through that all was not going to plan mrs smith explained that candidates were certainly experiencing problems as the systems had crashed in her opinion it would be better to extend the closing date would he be prepared to authorize this

Did you have any problem deciphering this? A lot of people will find it difficult. If we write poetry we may actively want people to work out meaning. We may even want them to create their own meaning; but this should not apply to business writing.

In writing, punctuation is an aid that helps our readers to understand our messages. The extract could be punctuated a number of ways. I will use one way to show how it becomes easier to read:

Mr Jones, the company's HR director, called Mrs Smith into his office for an update on the latest recruitment drive. He wanted to know whether the online application system was working. Reports had filtered through that all was not going to plan.

Mrs Smith explained that candidates were certainly experiencing problems as the systems had crashed. In her opinion, it would be better to extend the closing date.

Would he be prepared to authorize this?

You see, punctuation and grammar are aids that help writing to be understood and help us to communicate clearly. A good command of these can give you improved confidence, and you can feel more in control of your business English writing. You will be pleased about this and so will your readers. You will feel secure in the knowledge that your sentences will work because you have designed them to work.

Punctuation and other marks

English terms and symbols used to describe punctuation marks are:

capital letters or upper case: A, B, C

lower case: a, b, c

comma: ,

full stop (UK English) or period (UK and US English) or dot: .

speech or double quotation marks or inverted commas: " "

speech or single quotation marks or inverted commas: ' '

question mark: ?

exclamation mark: !

apostrophe: '

hyphen or dash: –

slash or stroke: /

brackets: ( )

square brackets: [ ]

ampersand: &

'at' sign: @

colon: :

semicolon: ;

asterisk: *

Nouns and gender in English

Nouns and pronouns in English belong to one of four genders: masculine, feminine, common (words denoting either sex) or neuter.

Examples of masculine nouns and pronouns are:

man, boy, father, brother, heir, lion, him.

Examples of feminine nouns and pronouns are:

woman, girl, mother, heiress, lioness, her.

Examples of common nouns and pronouns are:

child, owner, officer, friend, they, you.

Examples of neuter nouns and pronouns are:

book, office, street, it.

The definite and indefinite article in gender

English differs from many other languages in that:

- The word 'the' (referred to as the 'definite article') is a constant. It does not change according to the gender of the word to which it relates.

- The words 'a' (referred to as the 'indefinite article') or the alternative form 'an' (used to precede a word that begins with a vowel) are also constants. They do not change according to the gender of the word to which they relate.

This should make life easy for non-native English writers – although they can have a tendency to default to their own language's convention. Some may refer to neuter English words as 'he' or 'she', which can sound very odd to native English speakers.

Another problem is the fact that, for almost every rule in English grammar, there is an exception. For example, a ship is generally referred to in English as 'she'. Cars can be referred to this way too. Yet a cat, dog or other animal can also be referred to as 'it' – and anything belonging to it would be 'its'. For example: 'Its feeding bowl is over there.' Very strangely, a baby can be referred to as 'it' too! For example: 'It's a cute baby', or 'Its feed is due now' (meaning 'The baby's feed is due now.').

Although I deal with apostrophes a bit later, I will just explain the difference in meaning between 'it's' and 'its' in the last paragraph. The apostrophe (') in 'it's' tells you that a letter is missing. In this case it is the letter i. So the meaning in this case is 'it is'. Sometimes the apostrophe will signify that two letters are missing. In that case the meaning will be 'it has'. The context will help you understand which of the two possibilities applies. When you see 'its' with no apostrophe (') between the t and the s, this meaning will always be 'belonging to it', 'owned by it', 'of it'. We call this the possessive or genitive case.

Parts of speech and other grammar

Parts of speech

In English grammar, words can be categorized into what we term parts of speech. These include nouns, pronouns, adjectives, verbs, adverbs, prepositions, conjunctions and interjections.

A noun names a person, place or thing. For example:

girl, London, newspaper;

The man drank his coffee.

A pronoun is a word that can take the place of a noun and functions like it. For example:

I, this, who, he, they;

There's Peter, who won the lottery.

You will notice how the noun 'Peter' became the pronoun 'who' within the same sentence.

An adjective is a word that describes a noun. For example:

red, lovely, clever;

That is a lovely photo.

A verb is a 'doing word' or describes a state of being. For example:

write, run, work, be;

She is an assistant who works hard.

Sometimes a verb needs two or three words to complete it. For example:

I am working in Moscow this week.

You will be travelling first class.

An adverb is a word that describes a verb. For example:

fast, happily, later, urgently;

The project manager always delivered on time.

In that last example there is an adverb, 'always', and an adverbial phrase, 'on time', which describe the verb 'delivered'.

A preposition is a word that links a noun to another noun. For example:

to, on, under, in;

Please put the papers on the desk.

A conjunction is a word that joins words or sentences. For example:

and, but, or, so;

I need a flipchart and paper, but that is all.

An interjection is a short exclamation, often followed by an exclamation mark (!). For example:

hi! oh!

Oh no! I've just missed the train.

Some other grammatical points of interest

Commas can separate one group of words in a sentence from another so that the meaning is clear. You will see how they flag up different meanings in these two sentences:

Sanjay, our vice-president has left the company.

Sanjay, our vice-president, has left the company.

In the first sentence, the writer is telling Sanjay that their vice-president (somebody else) has left the company. In the second sentence, the writer is telling somebody (whose name is unknown to us) that Sanjay (who is the vice-president) has left the company.

In order to use commas correctly, it helps to know that a comma signifies a brief pause. Very often, people wrongly use a comma to do the work of a full stop (period). For example:

I examined the computer, it had obviously been damaged.

As there are two complete statements here, not just a pause, a full stop is appropriate: 'I examined the computer. It had obviously been damaged.' However, this sounds rather stilted and a native English writer is likely to use a conjunction to add fluidity. For example: 'I examined the computer and found it had obviously been damaged.'

A comma is also used to link lists of items, groups of words, adjectives, actions and adverbs. For example:

She listed, there and then, the things she would need for her presentation: a laptop, a projector, screen, flipchart and marker pens.

Apostrophes show where one or more letters have been left out of a word. For example:

I'm = contraction of 'I am';

It's = contraction of 'it is' or 'it has';

You'll = contraction of 'you will'.

Apostrophes can also show possession or ownership. For example:

The student's rights = the rights of one student;

The students' rights = the rights of students.

The general rule is:

apostrophe before the s ('s) = singular possession;

apostrophe after the s (s') = plural possession.

Unfortunately, English always has some irregular forms, such as:

men = plural of man; but the possessive is men's;

children = plural of child; but the possessive is children's;

its = possessive of it – yet takes no apostrophe at all!

Forming plurals of nouns

As you will know, most nouns have a singular form (to denote one) and a plural (to denote more than one). There are exceptions that I have highlighted earlier, such as training and information. The standard way of forming plurals from singular nouns is to add 's'. However, this does not always work, as in the case of 'child, children', 'lady, ladies', 'foot, feet', to mention a few. So please do refer to a mainstream English grammar book if you need more help with this.

There is one point that I would like to address here, as it arises so often. It concerns the wrong use of an apostrophe followed by 's' to signify a plural meaning. For example, 'tomato's' and 'company's'. The correct plurals are 'tomatoes' and 'companies'.

Vowels and consonants

In written English, 'a, e, i, o, u' are the standard vowels. The remaining letters in the alphabet are consonants.

The definite and indefinite article

The word 'the' is known as the definite article and exists in the same form in both singular and plural. The words 'a' and 'an' are known as the indefinite article and only exist in the singular. For the plural, English uses the word 'some'.

If as a non-native English writer you are sometimes confused about when to use the definite or indefinite article, you are definitely not alone. A general guideline that will help is this. When you are referring to something in general, use 'a' before a word beginning with a consonant or 'an' before a word beginning with a vowel. (Once again though, true to form, English has exceptions: some native English speakers would say 'an hotel'.)

Here is an example of 'a' in this usage:

> Cheese for sale: six euros a kilo, *not* 'six euros the kilo', as many non-NE writers would expect.

As an interesting aside, note that in English goods are described as being 'for sale'. Some cultures express it the reverse way: 'to buy'. English speakers would say and write 'House for sale', not 'House to buy'.

Let's say a company receives an e-mail as follows: 'Please can you let me know how long an order will take to deliver?' The company will view the question posed as tentative – and thus non-specific. There is no order, only a general enquiry about how long it would take if somebody did place an order. Now let's say the company receives this e-mail enquiry: 'Please can you tell me how long the order will take to deliver?' The word 'the' makes this enquiry far more specific. The question is more likely to relate to an order that has been placed.

Paragraphs

Paragraphs help your reader understand the organization of your writing because each paragraph is a group of sentences about a topic. Your key messages become easy to identify and the format makes it easy for you to develop them. Paragraph headings are increasingly used to signpost messages and highlight structure for readers' ease.

Brackets, bullet points and dashes

Use these to break up text (especially if it is rather lengthy) so that your reader is not overwhelmed – you will find they can be really useful. Can you see from the last sentence that I used a dash (–) for a similar purpose? You can also use commas, as I am doing here, to make a longish sentence more manageable. It also acts as a point of emphasis: the main message is in the main part of the sentence, and the aside is within the commas or brackets.

On the reverse side, too many short sentences can seem abrupt. So if you want to keep your writing interesting, try mixing and matching these features to vary and enhance your style.

Verbs and tenses

You are likely to have been taught the finer points of English grammar at school, in college or by self-study. Needless to say, entire books are written on this extensive subject and it is beyond the scope of this handbook to go into any great detail. However, I will give an outline as a refresher.

As I have mentioned, a verb is a 'doing' or 'state of being' word. It can consist of one or more words. The infinitive of a verb is the base form, for example 'to work', 'to give', 'to do'.

The present participle is formed by adding '-ing' to the infinitive. The 'to' part is dropped. This construction is then used with the verb 'to be' to form what are known as continuous tenses. For example: 'They are working.'

If the infinitive ends in 'e' ('to give', 'to come') the general rule is to drop the 'e' when adding the '-ing'. For example: 'He is giving,' 'They are coming.'

The past participle is normally formed by adding '-ed' to the infinitive. Again, the 'to' part is dropped. This construction is used with the verb 'to have' to form perfect (completed past) tenses. For example: 'The train has departed,' 'The post has arrived.'

Irregular verbs form the perfect differently. That is why you may need to refer to traditional grammar sources if you are not sure about these. Examples are: 'It has grown' (not grow-ed), 'The time has flown by' (not fly-ed).

Tenses

The simple tenses in English are the starting point for global business writing today.

The present tense has the same form as the infinitive (except the verb 'to be'). When the subject is 'he', 'she', 'it' or a noun, English adds '-s' or '-es'.

To form the future tense, English adds 'will' (or 'shall' – though this is less frequently used now).

To form the past tense, '-ed' is normally added to the infinitive. (Once more though, a word of caution: there are many irregular verbs where this does not work!)

A regular example is:

verb: to work (regular verb)

simple present tense:

- I work

- you (singular and plural) work

- he, she, it works

- we work

- they work

simple future tense:

- I, you (singular and plural), he, she, it, we, they will work

simple past tense:

- I, you (singular and plural), he, she, it, we, they worked

There are naturally many more tenses that you will need to study in depth and dedicated grammar books will help you with the necessary detail involved. That said, there is one tense that does seem to present a particular problem in the workplace. Businesses ask me about this one so often that I think it merits a special mention here. It is the present continuous tense.

This tense is formed by using the present tense of 'to be' with the present participle of the verb in question. Let's say I want the present continuous tense of 'to write'. The forms are:

I am writing

you (singular and plural) are writing

he, she is writing

we are writing

they are writing

The question I am often asked is: when do we use the present continuous rather than the present tense? The answer is in three parts:

- When the action is taking place now ('I am writing this sentence at this very moment.').

- When the action is taking place now but also is carrying on into the future ('I am writing this book at this very moment – but also over the coming months.').

- When the action is planned for the future ('I am writing another book next year.').

By the way, with regard to this last sentence, you would be right to think that the future tense would also be correct, namely: 'I will write another book next year.'

We use the present tense for more general actions or states that have no particular time reference. For example:

We drink water to survive.

If I find a mistake, I correct it.

Non-native English writers can be confused about when to write, for example:

She lives in Tokyo.

She is living in Tokyo.

Both are correct – but the second version often implies to a native English speaker that 'She is living in Tokyo (at the moment).'

Agreement of subject and verb

When a subject in a sentence is in the singular, then the verb must be in the singular too. When the subject is plural, then the verb is in the plural, in agreement with it. This is also called concord. Examples are:

Paul is at university and so is his brother.

Paul is at university and so are his brother and sister.

They understand the reason why they have to do this.

She understands the reasons why she has to do this and why you have to do it too.

These conditions apply now.

This condition applies now.

Non-NE writers can forget to check concord in their writing. Two quite typical examples are:

Sara has received our e-mail. Has you received it too? Correct version: Sara has received our e-mail. Have you received it too?

This kind of topics. Correct version: These kinds of topics.

As a rule of thumb, all you have to do is work out who is doing the action and make your verb relate to who or what is doing it. In some sentences you may have to refer back to check.

   Incidentally, there are certain words in English where it is possible to use a singular word in a plural sense too. Examples are: government, council, committee, company.

So in UK English, you can write:

The government is changing the law on this.

The government are changing the law on this.

The reasoning behind this is that these nouns can be viewed as entities by themselves or as bodies of people. On this track, another often-used word comes to mind. This is the word 'staff', where it means personnel. It is used as a singular in US English but exists only in the plural in UK English. So UK English says: 'The staff are taking a vote on this.' US English says: 'The staff is taking a vote on this.'

Question tags

These are used a lot in English conversation, and non-NE speakers can find them quite hard to master. As they are now used in e-mail writing too, here are some tips.

Speakers and writers use question tags to encourage their listeners or readers to respond. It helps check that people agree or understand what you are saying or writing.

Examples are:

It's a good outcome, isn't it?

You don't have a meeting today, do you?

You can make it in time, can't you?

Examples of incorrect usage would be:

You have got the right files, isn't it?

He is wrong, doesn't he?

These kind of things are dealt with in your department, isn't it?

Correct versions of these would be:

You have got the right files, haven't you?

He is wrong, isn't he?

These kinds of things are dealt with in your department, aren't they?

Tips to help you:

Try balancing the same verb (including whether it is singular or plural) on either side of the sentence.

Then use a negative in the end questioning part of the sentence.

Comparison

Comparison of adjectives

In English, adjectives can have three degrees: positive, comparative and superlative.

The positive is just the usual form of the adjective; for example: a happy child, a large book, a comfortable chair.

The comparative is used in comparing one thing or group with another; for example:

the shorter of the two brothers;

ponies are smaller than horses.

If it is a short word, we normally form the comparative by adding '-er'.

The superlative is used when comparing one thing or group with more than one other; for example:

She is the oldest of the three sisters.

That is the greatest suggestion yet.

If it is a short word, we normally add '-est' to the positive.

Adjectives of three syllables or more and most adjectives of two syllables form their comparative by placing the word 'more' before the adjective. They form the superlative by placing 'most' in front of the adjective.

Some adjectives have quite different words for the comparative or superlative. For example:

good, better, best;

many, more, most;

little, less, least.

Incidentally, a mistake that is very common is where writers use the superlative where they should be using the comparative. For example: 'That is the best of the two offers' is, strictly speaking, wrong. It should be: 'That is the better of the two offers.' There would have to be three or more offers for 'best' to be correct. Similarly, instead of 'She is the youngest of the two employees', the correct version would be 'She is the younger of the two employees.'

Comparison of adverbs

Short adverbs are compared in the same way as adjectives:

soon, sooner, soonest;

fast, faster, fastest.

With adverbs of two syllables or longer, you usually form the comparative and superlative by adding 'more' and 'most' to the positive degree of the word:

carefully, more carefully, most carefully;

easily, more easily, most easily.

Once again, English often comes up with irregular forms:

badly, worse, worst.

well, better, best.

Transitional words and phrases

Let's now take a look at transitional words and phrases which can play a useful part in improving fluidity in writing.

You may feel you have succeeded in your writing if you have included all the points you need to make. You would be right, up to a point. But successful outcomes can be very much based on whether we get the reactions and replies we need from our readers. If our writing is not fluid and well thought through, readers may not be bothered to make an effort to find out more. This presents at least three further, highly undesirable, outcomes:

1.   Readers may walk away and go elsewhere for answers (this can be either internally or externally. If externally, it means lost business and lost goodwill; if internally, it means loss of face and goodwill.

2.   They may not take the required action.

3.   They may take the wrong action.

Transitional phrases help us show the relationships between one idea or statement and subsequent ones. They can link paragraphs, point towards a bigger picture and can help lead readers to a logical conclusion. Some transitional phrases (categorized by heading) are:

Addition:

- and;

- besides;

- in addition;

- also;

- equally important;

- furthermore;

- what's more;

- similarly;

- first;

- second (etc);

- finally.

Comparison and contrast:

- but;

- yet;

- however;

- on the one hand;

- on the other hand;

- while;

- although;

- compared to;
- nevertheless;
- whereas.

Example:
- for example;
- for instance;
- as an illustration;
- take the case of;
- in this situation.

Purpose:
- with this in mind;
- so;
- since;
- clearly;
- for the same reason;
- that is;
- indeed.

Result or conclusion:
- because of this;
- so;
- thus;
- finally;
- in conclusion;
- consequently;

- as a result;

- summing up.

There are many more categories and it could be really worth-while for you to research this topic further. Fluidity when writing English for business pays great dividends: you provide the links so that the reader does not have to work them out. This next example illustrates how.

> ABC Ltd is a well-established manufacturing company founded in 1999 that has decided to go for growth in its next five-year plan.
> **Despite** a downturn in the manufacturing sector generally, ABC has identified two principal ways of maintaining a successful business.
> **First**, management has changed the structure of the business by splitting its commercial department into two entities: sales and production. **Second**, it has introduced a new outcome-based approach to assessment, which involves staff to a greater degree than before.
> **As a result**, the company has significantly improved profits **as well as** winning a prestigious customer service award.

Your checklist for action

- Present facts clearly and present a well-argued, well-supported business case.

- Write so that readers do not have to make an effort to understand you or come back to you for further in-formation, or wait for you to make things clear.

- Write so that readers are more likely to take a favourable view of you.

- Punctuation serves the useful purpose of helping readers read messages; and it highlights where the emphasis needs to go.

- Grammar helps you set out business writing into manageable sections that help readers understand your meaning.

- Identify areas of punctuation and grammar to work on.

- Fluidity helps you set out the points in a coherent way. All the points you make add up. Two and two are seen to make four in your writing, not just in your sums.

7

Writing tips for everyday business

Writing a date

Differing conventions

It is important to realize that there are a number of correct ways of writing dates in English. The UK English format (which most of Europe uses) is:

DD / MM / YY, where D = day, M = month, Y = year.

This is in sharp contrast with the US format, which is:

MM / DD / YY.

And both are in contrast with the format used in Japan, for example, which is:

YY / MM / DD.

Not understanding the different conventions can create immense problems. If you have to book international transport or hotel accommodation, or arrange deliveries, meetings and so on, you will know how important it is to input the correct dates. It can simply be a question of house style regarding the format you choose to be your default convention. However, you may need to be flexible and understand that customers may be using a different convention. Check if there's any uncertainty. Sometimes be prepared to mirror their convention, as long as it's an acceptable version that makes sense. Being in business should be about embracing customers' needs, not about seeing them as 'awkward' if they do something differently.

Examples that are all perfectly acceptable in UK English are:

21 January 2009;

21st January, 2009;

21 Jan 2009;

21st Jan 2009;

21/01/09.

If your house style uses the format '1st, 2nd, 3rd', you may have spotted that the abbreviation is based on the spoken or written version of the word in question. So 1st stands for 'first', 2nd for 'second', 3rd for 'third', and so on – placing the final two letters of the abbreviated word behind the number.

As I mentioned, US English uses a month / day / year format, as do some other countries. In this case, you would write:

January 21 2009;

01/21/09.

This particular date is not too problematic because we know that there are not 21 months in a year. But where readers do not understand the differences between the UK and US conventions, they could have problems with a date such as 03/06/09. In the UK this denotes 3 June 2009, but in the US it denotes 6 March 2009.

International date format

This has been devised to make the way we write dates internationally understandable. It is based on the following format:

YYYY – MM – DD.

In this format, YYYY refers to all the digits (eg 2015), MM refers to the month (01 to 12) and DD refers to the day (01 to 31).

When there is any doubt, it is really useful to write your dates in English this way.

Reading written dates out loud

If you have to read a written date out loud, I would suggest you say, for example, 'the twenty-first of January, two thousand and nine'. But in normal office correspondence, nobody would expect me to write 'the 21st of January 2009'. The place you might see this type of writing is in a legal document such as a contract.

Days of the week

In English, if you want to indicate the actual day of the week you can write either the full word or its abbreviation. For example:

Monday, Mon;

Tuesday, Tues;

Wednesday, Wed;

Thursday, Thurs;

Friday, Fri;

Saturday, Sat;

Sunday, Sun.

The formal convention is always to use a capital letter for the first letter of each day of the week. Do note that some writers punctuate the abbreviation with an end full stop or period; for example, Tues. This convention is optional.

Take particular care over the spelling of Wednesday. Even native writers can have a problem with this one!

Months and their customary abbreviations

January, Jan;

February, Feb;

March, Mar;

April, Apr;

May (never abbreviated);

June, Jun (but rarely abbreviated);

July, Jul (but rarely abbreviated);

August, Aug;

September, Sept;

October, Oct;

November, Nov;

December, Dec.

Do note:

- The first letter of each month is written as a capital.

- Some writers punctuate the abbreviation with a full stop at the end, but modern business practice tends to be to omit this.

Some confusions

Days and weeks

If you write 'next Tuesday', people can get confused as to whether you are referring to the first Tuesday that follows after the day you wrote this – or whether you mean a Tuesday in another week. So, as an example, if you write it on a Monday, is 'next Tuesday' the following day (which I would take it to mean), or the Tuesday of the following week? If you write it on a Friday, it is easier to see that it would have to be the Tuesday of the following week.

'This coming Tuesday' has the same meaning as 'next Tuesday'. So do be careful. I know of instances where misunderstandings about this have led to missed appointments. Ironically, the people who misunderstand the correct use of the expression are the ones who can get angry. Also, imagine the cost if you book foreign travel for the wrong date. The best arrangement is always to write the precise date you mean, for example: 'next Tuesday, 4th November'.

'In a couple of weeks' literally means 'in two weeks', as 'couple' means 'two' in English. It is true that 'a couple of weeks' can be used in a looser sense, meaning in about two weeks, but it is best to check. As another example, the Dutch expression '*paar dagen*' means a few days, but the Dutch often wrongly translate this into English as 'a couple', or 'two' days. So where orders are concerned, it is best to clarify what is meant in these instances.

'Next Monday week' means 'a week from next Monday'. 'Over a week' in English means 'in more than a week's time'. But non-NE writers often use the expression 'over a week' to mean in a week's time, that is, one week from now. An example would be: 'The delivery will be over a week.' Again be careful if you are dealing with orders, because you can confuse.

'A fortnight' means two weeks. I find that many national-ities are unaware of this word, so it can be better to avoid it.

'A long weekend' means a break of three or four days that includes a Saturday and Sunday, and may start on a Friday and end on the following Monday.

Time off

In UK English, people usually refer to their 'holidays' where US English uses 'vacation'. Time off work for holidays is referred to as 'leave'; time off through illness is 'sick leave'; parents' time off from work when a baby is born is either 'maternity leave' (for the mother) or 'paternity leave' (for the father).

Time off work may be 'paid leave' or 'unpaid leave', de-pending on circumstances.

Public and Bank holidays

A public holiday is an official holiday for the majority of a state or country. In the UK, the term 'Bank holiday' is used when the public holiday falls on a weekday when banks are closed by law.

When you write about public holidays or Bank holidays globally, be aware that they can vary from country to country, usually being cultural in origin.

Time

This is a topic that you absolutely must understand how to write correctly in English. Things can go seriously wrong when different nationalities fail to understand that they may have differing conventions for writing times. People fail to turn up to meetings at the right time, they miss flights, deadlines ... in short, if a matter is time bound it can go wrong. And what in business is not linked to time? Here are some guidelines to help.

UK English

All these written versions are correct in English:

The meeting starts at 09.00.

The meeting starts at 9am (or 9 am or 9 a.m.).

The meeting starts at nine o'clock in the morning.

The meeting starts at nine in the morning.

English usage includes both the 12-hour clock (morning and afternoon) and the 24-hour clock (especially for timetables), so:

09.00 means nine o'clock in the morning;

21.00 means nine o'clock in the evening.

Strangely enough, 24.00 is also 0.00 hours!

If we write in English, 'The meeting starts at half past eight,' this could mean 'The meeting starts at 08.30 or 20.30.'

Often we will know from context which is correct. For example, if meetings are held during normal office hours, then half past eight in the morning is the more likely time. But say we work in a staggered-hours environment, then it could be a morning or an evening meeting. You need to clarify.

Differing conventions in different countries

Mishaps or missed meetings and other appointments all arise when we fail to realize that the way different countries express time is not standard. For example, the USA does not generally use the 24-hour clock (except specifically by some professions: for example, the military, the police, the medical profession). Some countries (such as Germany and the Netherlands) use a format to express half an hour before an hour. This is alien to native English writing – where half past six, for example, should be expressed as 'half seven' to the German or Dutch way of thinking.

Do not underestimate how problematic failing to appreciate this source of misunderstanding can be. You need to ensure that everyone understands how to write and read times in English, for the sake of efficiency.

Numbers

If you are writing numbers in English, also be aware that different nationalities may interpret the numbers differently. Look how your order books could be affected – and your bottom line. For example, the words 'billion' and 'trillion' can have completely different meanings in the UK, Germany, France and the USA.

But a zillion means a large indeterminate number, so that expression at least is standard!

A fairly old imperial expression you will still find on occasion is dozen. It means 12.

You use a comma when you write a number comprising four or more digits. Counting from right to left, you place the comma after each three digits:

1,000;

10,000;

100,000;

100,000,000.

How the decimal point is written in English

'Decimal point' is the UK English term for the dot placed after the figure that represents units in a decimal fraction: for example, 9.6.

This may differ from the way you express the decimal point in your language. You may be used to using a comma – for example, 9,6 – or you may express 100,000,000 as 1000.000.000. It's not overly confusing but it is best to be aware of this difference when you write in English.

Decimal points when writing monetary units in English

Some nationalities express their decimal currencies using commas where there is a decimal fraction: €1,80.

If you are writing a tariff in English, you express this amount as: €1.80

Other punctuation differences are apparent in the following written representation of the same number. The UK English version is the first of these:

890,123.50

890.123,50

Measurements

Do you have to write measurements in English? If you are writing globally, do be aware that different countries use different systems. Broadly speaking, these are called metric and imperial.

The US largely uses imperial and the UK and other countries may use a combination. You will need to research if you are involved in orders that use either system. To give you an idea, some of the differences are as follows:

Metric system:

- length: centimetre, metre, kilometre (US spelling: meter etc);

- weight: gram, kilogram, tonne;

- capacity: millilitre (ml), litre (US spelling liter etc);

- temperature: Centigrade or Celsius.

Imperial system:

- length: inch, foot, yard, mile;

- weight: ounce, pound, ton;

- capacity: fluid ounce, pint, gallon;

- temperature: Fahrenheit.

Even within the imperial system, you will find that a US ton is not the same as a UK ton, and a US gallon is different to a UK gallon.

Temperatures are also written using different systems:

Centigrade or Celsius: freezing point of pure water 0° (degrees); boiling point 100°;

Fahrenheit: freezing point of pure water 32°; boiling point 212°.

How to write addresses (general)

I deal with addressing letters and envelopes in Chapter 10. An aspect I would like to mention here is that UK English uses the expression postcodes (or postal codes) where US English refers to zip codes for area codes within a city, county or country. These codes are not used in all countries.

Your checklist for action

- When writing dates, times and measurements, one size does not fit all.

- Understand the conventions used by the person to whom you are writing.

- If you do not do this, you may miss appointments and delivery deadlines etc.

- Your order books may be adversely affected if you get dates, times and numbers wrong – your profits too.

- Write as precisely as possible to avoid misunderstandings: for example, 2nd January 2012.

8

Common confusions and how to avoid them

Common confusions for both NE and non-NE writers

There are some words that repeatedly cause businesses confusion. In many cases the confusion arises because different people within the same company may be setting their computer spellcheck to different varieties of English. Other confusions can arise from homophones. These are words that have the same sound but can have different meanings and spellings.

Words or spellings that commonly confuse

I now list some commonly confused words together with examples of correct usage.

Programme (UK) and program (US)

'A programme' is a plan of events, a radio or television broadcast or coded software instructions for a computer or other machine. But within the UK you will find many writers using 'program' when referring to computer software.

Receive and recieve

The correct version is 'receive'. A useful rule in English spelling is that after the letter 'c' the letter 'e' goes before 'i'.

Stationary and stationery

'Stationary' means standing still: for example, 'The careless driver crashed into a stationary car.'

'Stationery' means writing and printing materials: for example, 'I have ordered new business stationery from my printer.'

Licence and license, practice and practise

In UK English, the nouns relating to these words end in '-ce'. The verbs end in '-se'. For example:

Which doctor's practice do you go to? (practice = noun = the doctor's place of work)

You should practise what you preach. (practise = verb)

In US English this difference does not exist. The '-ce' ending can apply to nouns and verbs. For example: 'He has a valid licence, so he is licenced to drive here.'

Remember and remind

'To remember' means to be able to bring something or someone back into your mind. For example: 'I must remember to update those details' (meaning: nobody else is involved).

'To remind' means to cause or prompt someone to remember something. For example: 'Please remind me to update those details.'

Affect and effect

'Affect' is a verb. For example: 'Recession affects spending.'

'Effect' can be a verb or a noun. For example: 'Recession has a negative effect on spending.'

'We must effect the changes.'

Compliment and complement

'Compliment' is a noun or verb meaning praising or admiring.

'Complement' is a noun or verb meaning a thing that completes something else. For example:

We are always delighted to receive a compliment from a customer.

When dining, the right ambience complements the meal.

Loose and lose

'Loose' is an adjective that means not tightly packed or fixed. For example: 'There is a loose connection in the wiring system.'

'Lose' is a verb that means cease to have, be unable to find. For example: 'If we lose their parcel we will also lose their custom.'

There and their

'There' is an adverb meaning in that place.

'Their' is an adjective meaning belonging to them. For example:

The file you need is over there.

It will be their turn next.

Where, were and we're

'Where' is an adverb, meaning in (or to) which place, direction or respect.

'Were' is a verb, the past tense of 'to be'.

'We're' is a contraction of 'we are'. For example:

Where are we going on holiday?

You were at home last night and now you are at work.

We're attending a training course today.

Your and you're

'Your' means belonging to you.

'You're' is the contraction of you are. For example:

Your bag is in the other room.

You're expected in half an hour.

Collect and pick up

In UK English 'collect' means to call for and take away, to fetch. The verb 'pick up' means the same. US English uses 'pick up' rather than 'collect' in this context.

Takeaway (or take-away) and carry-out

In UK English 'takeaway' (or take-away) is a restaurant or shop selling food to be eaten away from the premises. In US English the term 'carry-out' is used for this.

When and if

Many non-native English (non-NE) writers have difficulty understanding the distinction between these two words. Generally speaking, 'when' means 'at which time' or 'in which situation' or 'during the time that'. It has a definite feel to it, even though it may be in the future.

'If', on the other hand, is more tentative and hypothetical. It introduces a situation that is conditional: it supposes something will happen that is likely to make something else happen. Examples are:

If my train is on time, I will be in Paris in two hours. (UK English)

When my train is on time, I will be in Paris in two hours. (Typical non-NE variant)

Native English writers would not tend to write the second sentence. They intuitively build in the conditional clause: if one thing happens (the train arrives on time), then the second thing will result (I will be in Paris in two hours). The second thing depends on the first.

Now see if you can identify which of the following sentences is 'more English':

If it's not a problem, I will visit you tomorrow.

When it is not a problem, I will visit you tomorrow.

It is the first sentence, based on the same reasoning: if the first condition is met (that it is not a problem) then the second thing will happen (I will visit you tomorrow).

Native English writers begin sentences with 'when' in situations such as: 'When my train arrives, I need (or I will need) to find carriage A.'

Here two situations are in parallel. The meaning is: 'At the same time as the train arrives (or immediately after) I need or will need to find carriage A.'

May and can

The verb 'can' in English is used to express ability or being allowed to do something. It is definite in meaning. For example:

I can speak Spanish = I am able to speak Spanish.

Juan's boss says he can have a day off = Juan's boss says he is allowed to have a day off.

The verb 'may' is used to express possibility. For example, 'I may learn Spanish or Mandarin Chinese but haven't decided yet' tells us that the speaker is not yet able to speak either language.

'May' is also used to ask permission in a polite way: for example, 'May I go with you?' or 'May I have a cup of coffee, please?' That said, it is quite normal for business peers to say or write 'Can we talk about this?' 'Can I attend the meeting?'

Should, must and have to

'Should', 'must' and 'have to' are verbs that convey obligation. In writing 'should' can be interpreted as weaker in meaning than 'must' or 'have to'. For example, if I write, 'You should always check your spelling before you send an e-mail' you might think I am just recommending this as good practice. You could see it as an option, not an obligation. On the other hand, if I write, 'You must always check your spelling before you send an e-mail,' then I am making it very clear that this is not an option; it is a directive. 'Have to' carries the same weight.

Borrow and lend

If you 'borrow' something you take and use something that belongs to someone else (on the understanding that you will return it). For example: 'As it's raining, please may I borrow your umbrella? I'll give it back to you tomorrow.'

If you 'lend' something you give something to someone else to use (on the understanding that they will return it.) For example: 'Has your pen broken? I'll lend you mine until you get a new one.' So you would be wrong to write: 'I need to write but my pen has broken. Can I lend yours?' The pen is not yours to give to someone else! You need to borrow it in order to use it.

Teach and learn

When someone teaches, they give knowledge or instruction about a subject to someone else. For example: 'I am teaching you some tips about writing English for business.'

When someone learns, they receive knowledge or instruction. For example: 'You are learning how to improve your writing.' So you would be wrong to write: 'Will you learn me how to write?' You are the only person who can carry out the act of learning! I can show you how you will learn, by teaching you.

Abbreviations and acronyms

Acronyms are intended to make business writing easier. They make an abbreviated word formed by the initial letters of other words or a compound noun. The idea is to make the subject easier to refer to and easier to remember.

When you use abbreviations and acronyms, write them in full at the first mention, then follow with the abbreviation in brackets: for example, Regional Development Agency (RDA). People tend not to do this when an acronym is very likely to be recognized internationally. An example would be the UN (United Nations). It does depend on your target audience. After that first explanation, you may just use the acronym in the text that follows.

By coincidence I have just received an e-mail referring to APAC populations. I imagined that the writer was referring to Asia Pacific populations ... but decided to see if there were other acronyms for APAC. There certainly are! I will list just some:

APAC: Asia and Pacific;

APAC: Asia Pacific Advisory Committee;

APAC: Aboriginal Political Action Committee;

APAC: All People Are Customers;

APAC: Atlantic Pilotage Authority Canada;

APAC: Association Professionnelle des Agents Commerciaux de France (Professional Association of Commercial Agents of France).

Each of these groups will no doubt have it that their target audience will absolutely, one hundred per cent, understand their acronym. But my experience as a consultant tells me otherwise!

It does seem to me, and I am not alone, that overuse of acronyms can create rather than solve a problem. Also, even where you explain an acronym at the outset of a document, it can help readers if you repeat the words in full from time to time. You will have noticed that although I explain the acronym 'non-NE' earlier in this book, I still write it in full – 'non-native English' – on many occasions, to help reinforce it for you.

Also note that overly casual abbreviations in writing – such as 'no probs' (for 'no problems') can annoy readers. They can find this sloppy, unprofessional and discourteous.

Incoterms

Some abbreviations and acronyms that you are likely to en-counter are 'incoterms'. These are commonly used trade terms in international trade. Two common examples are FOB (free on board) and EXW (ex works).

Incoterms were first published by the International Cham-ber of Commerce (ICC) in 1936 and have been regularly up-dated since. They were devised because parties to a contract were not always aware that terms and abbreviations used could have different implications in different countries. If you deal with sales and marketing and/or arranging transportation of goods to overseas markets, do research this topic further. You may care to visit the ICC website, as the terms can be subject to copyright, so you need to enquire about their use. Sellers and buyers need to know both obligations and risks. Using the right standard expressions for each market avoids misunderstandings and possible litigation.

Active and passive

As most companies today favour the active over the passive voice in business writing, it is important that you understand the difference.

The active voice is where the subject does the action. Sentences that show this are:

The committee took action as a result.

The secretary handed the notes to the director.

The passive voice is where the subject of the active clause becomes secondary, where it is acted upon or receives the action. Often the word 'by' is added, as we can see in the following sentences:

Action was taken by the committee as a result.

The director was given the notes by the secretary.

In both these examples, we can still see the subjects (the committee and the secretary respectively) but they are easier to see in the active sentences, as they appear first. That alone is why it is better practice to use the active voice in business writing. But there are other reasons why active writing is better. The following, very typical, example of passive writing demonstrates this: 'A decision was taken to take the matter further.'

When readers see a sentence such as this, they can be utterly confused. Who took the decision? In operational terms, what happens next? That is a problem; we cannot know from the context. We need more information – yet experience shows that people often do not ask for that information.

Nominalization

Another continuing theme in this series concerns a mistaken belief held by many business writers. They think they must embellish or over-complicate their writing. Even when they speak articulately and get to the point effectively, they seem to feel that to write simply and clearly is a sign of weakness.

Sometimes they cannot break away from old habits where they correlate high and complex word count with high intellectual performance. Historically, academic writing, for example, uses nominalization, in which nouns are used in place of verbs. This can serve a useful purpose in writing about concepts. But in business it can make for pomposity and annoy readers. It can obscure messages and use up valuable time for writer and reader alike.

Here are some examples. The nominalization form is first, followed by the clearer verb form:

give clarification on this = clarify this;

in recognition of the fact = recognizing that;

during the installation process = when installing;

we are involved with negotiations = we are negotiating.

The verb form gives more energy: we know that something is happening in each case and that people are involved. See the contrast with nominalization, where users appear to hide behind language. That is never a great idea in business.

Your checklist for action

■ Be aware of the common confusions described in this chapter.

■ Do not assume that your reader knows the common terms or abbreviations you use, so write in a way that everyone will understand.

■ Define the terms you will be using and check that your readers use the same ones.

■ Make sure you write plain English, using words precisely.

■ Use active rather than passive writing where appropriate.

9

E-mail

General

E-mail is by far the predominant form of business writing today; indeed, inestimable billions of e-mails are sent worldwide each day. Even if we disregard the high percentage of spam that may be filtered out, the numbers received far eclipse the number of letters sent. Conservative estimates suggest that upwards of 75 per cent of our business writing is e-mails – yet very few companies offer training (let alone specific advice) on how to do this.

Let's just take a look at your business. How many e-mails in English do you write in a week at work? Do you treat them all as professional, corporate communication? If you hesitate, the chances are that you do not. This then raises the question: if not, why not? Your readers (customers) and your competitors may be ahead of you on this. Also, do you check each time you use e-mail that it is the right medium? Would a phone call or face-to-face conversation do the job more effectively?

It is apparent that overuse of e-mail creates a great deal of inefficiency in the workplace. There is little doubt that we are also losing many traditional problem-solving skills as a direct result. It is becoming such a pressing business concern that I need to mention it here.

When it comes to writing e-mails in English for global business, other factors need to be addressed as well. Non-native English writers often write over-concisely, to minimize the risk of making mistakes, though this can be at the cost of not making complete sense. And if your formatted message is to be transmitted to a hand-held device (for example, Blackberry or smartphone), then it can be indecipherable when your chosen features such as font, colours, bullet points, italics, underlining or use of bold have all been lost.

As e-mails are rapidly replacing letters, it is essential to maintain standards in these. They are equally important and equally part of your corporate communication.

The rise and rise of e-mail

I posed questions in the last section because you need to understand how to use and write for this fast-growing medium. Two fundamental findings emerge:

- E-mails are written by virtually all levels of staff in all types of company. Largely gone are the days of the traditional secretary: in a sense we are almost all secretaries while we are at work. If we are writing English in business, we generally have to design our writing ourselves.

- Looking at the statistics, it's easy to see how such vast e-mail usage can lead to information overload. Therefore it is crucial to maintain quality and make things as easy as possible for the reader, so that your e-mails stand out –

and for the right reasons rather than because your English is wrong.

E-mail scenarios to watch out for

Sending too quickly

We all do it: we type our messages and we click on the send button without checking them first. Speed of response can seem like a great idea but can create particular problems if you are a non-native English writer writing in English. Spelling and grammar mistakes, abrupt tone, overreacting or simply not answering questions can all make readers judge your e-mails in a negative light. Take the time you need to get it right.

Draft folder

So if you are really pressured and know you cannot complete your e-mail in English by return, think about drafting a reply. Move it into your draft folder until you can complete it, maybe after asking someone who is fluent in English for help.

CC or cc

This stands for 'carbon copy'. Not every non-native English speaker knows what it means. The cc field is for copying your e-mail to other recipients so that they see the same message as the main addressee. If you use a cc internally within your company, it's not generally a problem when those listed in the cc field see others' e-mail addresses. But where your cc field includes the e-mail addresses of external recipients, you may get into trouble because of privacy and data protection laws. Spammers can also use these lists – and forwarded e-mail addresses can harbour viruses.

BCC or bcc

This stands for 'blind carbon copy'. It means that the copy of the e-mail message is sent to a recipient whose address cannot be seen by other recipients. This is useful where confidentiality is required.

Multi-lingual and other e-mail threads

When it comes to business communication, there is nothing more frustrating, confusing or even downright rude than someone e-mailing you a message you literally cannot understand! Just because you are both corresponding in English, it is not suddenly going to mean that your recipient understands your language. This might seem obvious, yet the widespread use of e-mail threads can make a mockery of this need for clarity.

Read the following e-mail thread starting from bottom to top, to see how a multi-lingual thread can lead to confusion.

De: Paul Lederer
À: Harry Brown
Objet : Lead Project A

Hi Harry
Pierre Marceau passed me your request. We've contacted Pilar Lopez as she's the project manager for this and you'll find her e-mail on this below.
Kind regards
Paul

From: Pilar Lopez
To: Paul Lederer
Subject: Lead Project A

Paul,
Consignalo para llamarme.
gracias
Pilar

De: Paul Lederer
À: Pilar Lopez
Objet : Lead Project A

Pilar,
I think you're probably the best person to deal with the question posed below. Am I right? I know that as you are new to the company, you have difficulty writing in English, so feel free to reply to this in Spanish as I'll understand.
Regards,
Paul

De: Pierre Marceau
À: Paul Lederer
Objet: Lead Project A

Paul,
Je n'ai pas les informations dont Harry a besoin. Peux-tu l'aider ?
Merci
Pierre

From: Harry Brown
To: Pierre Marceau
Subject: Lead Project A

Hi Pierre,
I understand you have the full brief on this global project and I'm wondering if you could e-mail this over to me for familiarization, please.
Many thanks,
Harry

If I tell you that Harry Brown speaks only English, can you see how unhelpful this thread is going to be? First of all, who is dealing with Harry's request? It seems to be being passed from one person to another but Harry does not know that. The fact that Pilar Lopez has ultimately helpfully suggested (in Spanish) that Harry call her, is not something he is going to see from the thread. After all, it is Pierre who understands Spanish, not Harry. Also, why is Pilar suggesting that he give her a call, when he had asked Pierre for details by e-mail?

How is Harry going to feel? Annoyed? Yes. Alienated? Yes. Is the matter resolved? No. Harry will have to make further enquiries. To avoid this alienation (of which the sender is normally unaware, as it is rarely intentional) you could try these alternatives:

■ Be both courteous and efficient by summarizing, in English, the main facts of the message thread.

■ Avoid multi-lingual threads altogether.

■ Therefore start each message afresh.

Embedding responses

Whether or not you embed responses can be a question of knowing how well this method works both for you and your recipients. Some people cannot imagine working any other way. For others it is actually stressful, especially where they are the people left to weave together perhaps five differing views, all embedded into their original e-mail.

Have you ever had to figure out what the overall picture is, at the end of a complicated trail of embedded messages? If you are dealing with messages in your native language it can be quite a challenge. Imagine then how much worse this will be where you have to try to interpret broken or variant English too. There comes a point at which embedding messages can become 'hiding messages'. Quit before you get to that point – and start a new e-mail!

This example shows you how tricky it can be to decipher embedded text. Let's say your e-mail asks four people in four different countries for their observations. You suggest they each embed their comments using a different colour. So Alexei in Russia chooses dark blue, Kentaro in Japan chooses teal, Cora in the Netherlands chooses red (and chooses to use capitals as well), and Carmen in Chile chooses brown.

Can you already see the problems that this course of action may present? It's going to become a very complicated procedure. I pity the originator who will have to try to draw the strands together to make sense. Surely it would be simpler to send a separate e-mail to each of the four? Incidentally, can you see why Cora's choice may lead to further complications? I know red is an auspicious colour in China and no doubt in other countries too. But be aware that in many countries, red embedded print is used to correct written mistakes or make criticisms. Readers may literally see a comment in red as a problem – even if it is actually meant to be helpful and positive.

Cora has also chosen to use capitals. According to accepted e-mail etiquette, capitals throughout an e-mail signify that you are SHOUTING. Cora's comments could then appear to be criticisms, although she may never realize this or the fact that she might be offending readers as a result. So please do evaluate when and how to embed messages and when to avoid this writing technique.

Structure your e-mails

E-mail is largely viewed as a form of communication that is halfway between conversation and formal business writing. Many people feel this means they can type their ideas:

■   in the English words that just occur to them;

■   in no particular order;

■   with no stated objectives;

■   with no attention to punctuation, grammar or any other quality control;

■   with no attention to layout.

Yet feedback repeatedly suggests that readers do not like reading solid blocks of text. What's more, if they don't like the look of a piece of writing, they may intuitively feel they are not going to like its content. This feeling can even go so far as to prevent them bothering to read it.

When it comes to our personal e-mail, and to the fast-growing world of blogging, we can relax to an extent. These are areas where we can let our writing just capture our thoughts, more or less exactly in the English in which they spill out (though we still have to observe the constraints of the law, including libel etc). Readers are more likely to have the time and the inclination to read our outpourings – but this approach is definitely best avoided for business e-mail.

So my tips apply even more if you are writing English for a cross-cultural audience. Use an easy-to-read font, design good layout and enter some carriage returns when you type, so that your words are not bunched up and thereby difficult to read.

Leave some white space by using paragraphs for new topics; people will thank you for it because, by and large, people like white space. Structure every e-mail to help readers (especially those who may not be proficient in English) see exactly what your points are and where the e-mail is leading: that is, its purpose and who does what and when.

If you do not make the purpose, the time frame and any call to action clear, then people might not respond. And, of course, if your e-mail has no purpose, then you should not write it!

Designing how you write e-mails

Here are some guidelines to help you structure your e-mails well.

Corporate communication

Is there a corporate style regarding layout? Do you have a corporate font? Is the font you use easily readable, such as Arial, Tahoma, and Verdana? Is the point size you use large enough? (12 point or above is often recommended). Don't just use lower case alone: corporate e-mail should still be in standardized English. Are you using your spellcheck and grammar check – and have you selected the correct variety of English?

Tone and appropriateness

Probably most reader complaints about e-mails relate to poor tone and inappropriate subject matter. Regarding the first point, be aware that you need to introduce the right tone for your target audience in each e-mail, as we have seen earlier.

Check whether you are using the right style of English:

- Is 'Hi' is the right opening salutation?

- Or should you use 'Hello' or 'Dear' followed by the recipient's first name or title and surname?

- Or is it sufficient simply to use their first name alone; for example: 'Paolo'? (Some would find this approach curt.)

While I find that most companies I work with do use 'Hi' as the default salutation, this is not a 'one size fits all' solution. When in doubt, using mirroring techniques can be useful in cross-cultural situations. By this I mean that, where feasible, you try replying to readers in a similar way to the way they address you.

Always remember that if you are not prepared to say a particular thing face to face, or if you would not be happy for other people to see your e-mail (including people you may not know about), then do not write it!

Use a good subject heading; refresh it regularly

Why do people fail to choose meaningful subject headings for their e-mails? 'Update on Project A at end of week 30' is always going to be a better heading than simply 'Project A'. But then what should you do in subsequent e-mails? Refresh the headings, so that your messages always reflect the current picture. For example, is it efficient to keep that heading about week 30 when you are actually discussing progress at week 40?

Yet ineffective writers do this sort of thing time after time. It can be because they are preoccupied with writing the correct English in the main body of text but overlook the fact that subject headings still have to be updated.

Regularly refresh e-mails

I have discussed the problems that can arise from multilingual e-mail threads. Let me just reinforce the message now: try to get into the habit of stopping e-mail threads, maybe after the third message. Start a new e-mail and if you need to carry information over, just recap the key points.

Before you send

■   Reread your e-mail and check that your communication in English is correct on every level.

■   Make sure it does not include previous e-mail threads that may not be appropriate to forward on to the new reader(s).

■   Have you included any attachments? Are they in English too?

■   If you have copied somebody in, have you explained why?

■   Is the subject heading good?

■   Is the e-mail easy to read (font style and size etc)?

After sending

Check after the event (a day, two days, a week) that you have achieved the outcome you want. Check that the English you have written has worked for your needs.

Your checklist for action

Before you press send, ask yourself:

- Is e-mail the right communication medium? Is your English fit for purpose? E-mail is corporate communication and your English has to be professional.

- If you are not prepared to say your message face to face or let it be seen by others, you should not send it.

- Would it be a problem for you or your organization if this e-mail is forwarded in its entirety to other people without your knowledge?

- Did you systematically read and cover the points in the e-mail to which you are replying?

- Have you run a spellcheck and grammar check, using the correct variety of English?

- Have you developed the right rapport with your readers and met their business and cultural expectations?

- Have you checked your meanings?

10

Letter writing

General

The way companies have to write business English for customers today varies greatly from the way they would have written years ago. It is essential to realize how customers' expectations have changed. As you have seen in earlier chapters of this book, you can (and must) innovate and discard some of the things you may have been taught years ago. Yet there are still certain conventions that you should follow for your letters to achieve your objectives.

First of all, identify the purpose of your letter and its possible impact on your reader:

- Is it to inform? If so, why?

- Is it to instigate action? If so, what? Who by? How? When by?

- How do you want the reader to feel when reading your letter? Can your tone assist this?

Second, identify the format. Do you use templates and a standard font? Has this been assessed for readability? For example, Arial, Tahoma, Times New Roman and Verdana (amongst others) can be more readable than some cursive fonts, especially for non-NE readers. How compatible is the font you use with other systems? Does the font size fall within the routinely used 10–15-point range? Many consider that 12 point offers optimum readability – though you still need to consider the needs of those with visual impairment and other needs, and adapt your writing accordingly.

Do you use a subject heading above your main text? Do you use a reference or code? An informative subject heading can engage your reader's attention from the start. It also helps you identify the point of your letter. Customize it if you can. Even the use of the word 'your', as in 'Re: your contract XYZ', is more reader-friendly than 'Re: contract XYZ'. (Incidentally, you do not need to use 'Re:' at all; it is a question of house style.)

Third, identify how well your letters work. Try to get in the habit of asking yourself questions such as these each time:

- Did I achieve the right result from this letter?

- Or was there a problem? Why was that? Was it because of the English I used? What should I have written?

- Did I get no result when I had expected one? Why was that? Should I use English differently next time I write?

An example of a letter asking for information

This series is not designed to give you writing templates, so what follows is just an outline example of writing a letter in English. Even within the UK there are differing conventions as to where to place the date and address on a letter, and what salutations and endings to use, amongst other considerations. Other countries will naturally have differing conventions too. So once again, one size does not fit all and you would need to adapt the outline according to your chosen house style.

How to set out a business letter in English

Your company name and contact details
Addressee's name and job title
Addressee's company or organization name
Number or name of building
Name of street or road
Post town
Postcode (UK addresses)
County, district or state
Area code or zip code (US addresses)
Country

Date

Reference number

Opening salutation (with or without a comma, depending on house style)

Heading

Main body of text

Closing salutation (with or without a comma, depending on house style)

Name of writer
Position in organization

Enc. (refers to enclosures, if there are any)

Now let's look at the outline in practice. This is quite a standard letter from one company to another, asking another for some further information regarding a proposed project.

Version 1

This is where the writer does not know the name of the person they are writing to:

The Managing Director
Trans-Continent Projects Ltd
21-24 Any Street
Anytown
AB3 4CD
UK

16 September 2009

Your reference: RP/01/1220

Dear Sir or Madam

Your proposed rail projects

We understand that you are launching several rail projects over the next 10 years and are looking for companies who can assist you.

As a company with leading expertise in this area, we would be very interested in the concession you propose to award a company for the design and implementation of the necessary railway tracks. For this reason, we would be grateful if you could forward us further details in this connection.

Yours faithfully

Per Smidt
Director
Smidt Holdings

Enc. Please find our company brochure enclosed, as an introduction to our company.

Note that 'Yours faithfully' is the UK English convention. In US English you will find such a letter could end with 'Sincerely' or 'Best regards' or 'Yours truly'. Note also that 'Yours faithfully' should be used in UK English only when you do not know the name of the addressee; see below for the convention to observe when you know their name.

Version 2

If you know the person's name you should use it in your opening salutation: for example, 'Dear Mr Smith' (or Mrs Smith, Ms Smith, Miss Smith). This is the formal use of their surname. Or you can write 'Dear Yusuf' (or Sara etc); this is the informal use of their first name. When you end the letter you write 'Yours sincerely' rather than 'Yours faithfully'.

Where possible, try to ascertain the name of the person to whom you are writing. Naturally, some situations will always stay formal and may even adhere to the 'Dear sir or madam' formula. But as relationship building can be crucial to business success, it is really worthwhile personalizing your letter writing.

Open punctuation

You or your company choose whether you use open punctuation in business letters today. This simply means that you can have a comma after the opening salutation ('Dear ...'), or you can omit it. And the same applies to your sign-off ('Yours ...'). But whichever option you choose, you should ensure that your usage is consistent in both the salutation and the sign-off.

Outline letter confirming a booking

The need to use different styles for different letters is highlighted elsewhere in this series. But you may find it helpful to see an example, this time just the main body of text of a letter. I have used a hotel example, as the language of global tourism tends to be predominantly English.

Dear Mrs Smith

We are pleased to confirm your reservation

Thank you very much for sending us details regarding your proposed stay. We are pleased to confirm the following reservation:

Guest: Mrs Jane Smith
Arrival date: 14 August 2009
Departure date: 16 August 2009
Number of rooms: 1
Room category: double room, non-smoking, first floor
Room rate: summer special as agreed, inc VAT
Reservation number: 007

Your credit card guarantees the room for you.

The room will be ready at 3.00 pm on the day of your arrival and remains at your disposal until 12.00 noon on the day of your departure. It is our policy to charge a 90% cancellation fee for no-show guests, but there is no charge where we receive your cancellation in writing within 24 hours before the date of your arrival.

We look forward to welcoming you to our hotel and hope you will have a very pleasant stay.

Yours sincerely,

Denis Paphides
General Manager
Hotel Beau Rivage

Note that in UK English 'ground floor' means the floor of a building at ground level. The first floor means the level (storey) above this. In many countries 'first floor' means the ground floor (US English observes this convention).

Stay ahead or stay behind

Although I have set out some standard formats, I demonstrate throughout this series of books that there is rarely just one correct style of writing in English. As circumstances change, we need to adapt and create new designs to work for us and for our readers.

Here is an extract from a letter that quite 'wowed' me when I first received it. It was a mailshot from a design agency.

Dear Mrs Talbot

How can I help?

We value our customers and we make it our duty to understand their needs and requirements so that we can help them to make their businesses work even better.

Can we do that for you?

Investing a small amount of your valuable time in a brief appointment is all that I ask of you to enable me to understand your business needs, and offer you helpful suggestions as to how you could reduce costs, at the same time as taking your business forward.

Yours sincerely
Signature and company name

Although there was not a great deal of text, I was impressed just by the look and feel of what was there. The simplicity of the message and the development of a two-way relationship (between me and them) made impact, especially as most companies were not writing that way at that time. This agency achieved this by using creative sub-headings and by writing 'I', 'we' and 'you' – and yes, it worked: I bought from them. It is an example of how innovative writing in English can win new business.

As I have said earlier, your teachers of English might have said, 'No, you can't write like that at work.' What I am saying is, 'Yes, actually, you can!' It can make all the difference between staying ahead in business and staying behind!

Specific tips about addressing letters

Always check the spelling of the name of the person you are writing to and their correct job title. We know that readers are quickly (and justifiably) offended when their personal details are incorrect. It can be difficult, though, if you do not know whether a foreign or unfamiliar name relates to a male or female. Ideally, make enquiries; maybe someone else will know. Or you could use the person's full name at the beginning of the letter – for example, 'Dear Chris Palmer' – to avoid embarrassment or offence.

Titles to use when addressing people

Standard titles used to address people in English are:

Mr (after which you write an adult male's name, whether single or married);

Master (after which you write a male child's name);

Mrs (after which you write a married female's name);

Ms (after which you write the name of an adult female who may or may not be married);

Miss (after which you write the name of a female child or an unmarried female).

Years ago, it was the practice to write 'Mr.' and 'Mrs.' punctuated with a period or full stop. This punctuation highlighted the fact that the words were abbreviations of the words 'mister' and 'mistress' respectively. Common practice today is to write both words with open punctuation: 'Mr' and 'Mrs' – without a full stop.

Another title in common use is 'Dr'. It is used for both male and female medical doctors, as well as for postgraduates with a Doctor of Philosophy degree (PhD or DPhil). So, for example, you write 'Dear Dr Smith', and there is no indicator whether Dr Smith is male or female. Some languages do build this in. For example, the German 'Herr Doktor' translates as 'Mr Doctor' in English, or 'Frau Doktor' translates as 'Mrs Doctor'. For some unknown reason, English does not make this distinction.

Take care to spell names correctly too. Get a name wrong and the chances are you will find out the hard way: your recipients may complain to you or about you. There may also be commercial implications if compliance-related documentation has wrong details. The repercussions can be serious and costly on many levels.

Addressing envelopes

When you send a letter, the envelope can be the first point of contact with the customer, especially if you mark it 'Personal'.

So be professional in the way you address it. We know people can return junk mail unopened. But sometimes there is mail that they need to see – yet they send this back unopened too, simply because their details are wrong on the envelope. They refuse to accept it until the sender corrects the mistakes.

You normally write addresses as follows:

Addressee's name and job title
Addressee's company or organization name
Number or name of building
Name of street or road
Post town
Postcode (UK addresses)
County, district or state
Area code or zip code (US addresses)
Country

CVs and covering letters

It is a good idea to have a regularly updated CV, even if you are not actually applying for another job. It helps you see the milestones you have achieved and the personal attributes you have enhanced. It also helps you see yourself as a brand: that is to say, what makes you special over and above the next person.

Here is a CV example you could adapt. It uses the UK and US convention, and starts with the person's current or most recent employment. Some countries expect the list to start with the earliest employment details and may expect different formatting.

Include only facts that can be verified, and make sure you accurately describe your personal attributes. You must be able to deliver what you say you can.

CV

John Smith

Home address: (ensure you use the correct style)
Telephone: (landline and mobile; include international dialling codes if necessary)
E-mail address: (details as appropriate)

Key strengths

Integrity and a strategic, creative thinker;

Logistics expertise at middle-manager level (able to give practical guidance covering legal, insurance and health and safety issues);

Strong verbal and written communication skills;

Clear time management and prioritization skills;

Responsive to change: help companies constantly to review operations and improve efficiency.

Career summary

October 2009 – present: XYZ Ltd Key Account Manager

Key achievements:

Secured and developed 30 new key accounts;

Successfully led process design, implementation and client relationship management arising from these;

Identified, advised on and managed new distribution business opportunities/ services.

July 2002 – September 2009: ABC Inc Project Manager

Key achievements:

Advised on and managed re-engineering services to meet changing needs and new service capabilities.

Professional membership

Affiliate Member of the Institute of Transport and Logistics

Education, training and other qualifications

(Fill in as appropriate, starting with most recent.)

Other skills

Computing: competent in Word, Excel, Outlook, PowerPoint;

Languages: fluent in English, Spanish and Russian;

Driving: clean current driving licence.

References

Available on request.

Note that UK English uses the term 'mobile' or 'mobile phone' where US English uses 'cell' or 'cellphone'. As I mentioned in Chapter 2, the term 'handy', which is used in continental Europe, is unlikely to be understood by most English speakers.

Covering letter with CV

When applying for a job, send a good covering letter with your CV, as this can improve your chances of getting to interview stage. Do not use a standard letter; customize it for your prospective employer. Make every effort to send the letter and your CV to the correct person, spelling their details and job title correctly, and to the right address.

Incidentally, you may have seen the expression 'To whom it may concern' and wonder when to use it. It is used where the writer does not know who the recipient will be. For example, if you are a contractor leaving one assignment, the company for whom you have worked may give you an open reference such as this:

To whom it may concern

Fred Jones designed and successfully implemented a software programme company-wide for us from June to September this year. He delivered the programme on time and within budget, and we found him to be a consummate professional at all times.

Gert Braun
Brunner BV

Once you have correctly addressed your letter, then:

- Say where you saw the job advertised.

- Show how you have done some research on the company (refer to something relevant on its website, such as its values).

- Answer the question 'Why should you get the job?' by highlighting the special skills you can bring.

- Mention any special factors that the company should take into account.

- Show what you expect from a prospective employer as much as what they can expect from you.

- State your availability.

■ Run a final spellcheck and grammar check; after all, if
English is required in the job, make sure yours is perfect
in your application!

Depending on culture and personality, people tend even in their
native language either to understate their suitability for any
vacancy being advertised or in some cases to over-embellish
it. The following non-native English writers' descriptions of
their suitability as job candidates definitely fall into the second
category:

> **An accountant:** 'I dispose of untouchable integrity and
> corresponding success and my brilliance is impressive.'
>
> **A marketing manager:** 'My knowledge, ratio and
> outstanding attributions decide that my future will be
> with your company.'

These are examples of what I term 'over-Englishing': the
desire to outdo native English writers with an exaggerated
use of language that deviates from the original. It is in essence
an imaginary language – and in the ultimate analysis, it has no
meaning. I could rewrite what I think they mean to say (and
this is not at all clear, probably not even in their own minds)
as follows:

> **An accountant:** 'A successful professional with integrity,
> I will be pleased to use my expertise in the post
> advertised.'
>
> **A marketing manager:** 'I am looking to take my career to
> the next level and have every confidence that my excellent
> credentials, expert knowledge and skills base will deliver
> what you seek in this post.'

Your checklist for action

- Know how to design a letter well.

- Know what you want the letter to achieve; enable the result you need.

- Write your recipient's personal details correctly.

- Use the correct salutation and sign-off.

- Edit so that the reader sees your key messages clearly.

- Build in rapport and politeness.

- Represent yourself and your company well.

- Do not make assumptions.

- Use spellcheck and grammar check (in the correct variety of English) before issuing your letter.

- Do not embellish or over-complicate your writing to create impact. It could work against you.

Conclusion

By now you will be feeling more confident about writing great English for today's business. And you will be more competent to do so. You will be closing the skill gap between where you were before you read the book and where you are now – and where you want to be.

Writing English for business is a key and – this is crucially important – a highly transferable skill. Carry on closing the gap, and see how many opportunities you will create for yourself. Take these tips on board, so that everything you write from now on is likely to be good – and you will actually keep on getting better. Congratulations on making a good start.

The Preface to this book explains how the series fits together. With this book and the others in the series you will have a comprehensive and invaluable reference guide for almost all aspects of your business English writing needs.